THE BIG HUSTLE

THE BIG HUSTLE

A BOSTON STREET KID'S STORY OF ADDICTION AND REDEMPTION

JIM WAHLBERG

FOREWORD BY JIM CAVIEZEL

Our Sunday Visitor
Huntington, Indiana

The views expressed throughout this book are solely those of the authors and do not necessarily represent the views of OSV.

Special thanks to Bill Kauffman for his assistance in preparing the manuscript for publication.

Except where noted, the Scripture citations used in this work are taken from the *Revised Standard Version of the Bible — Second Catholic Edition* (Ignatius Edition), copyright © 1965, 1966, 2006 National Council of the Churches of Christ in the United States of America. Used by permission. All rights reserved.

Our Sunday Visitor Publishing Division
Our Sunday Visitor, Inc.
200 Noll Plaza
Huntington, IN 46750
www.osv.com
1-800-348-2440

ISBN: 978-1-68192-603-2 (Inventory No. T2468)
1. BIOGRAPHY & AUTOBIOGRAPHY—Rich & Famous.
2. BIOGRAPHY & AUTOBIOGRAPHY—Personal Memoirs.
3. SELF-HELP—Substance Abuse & Addictions—Drugs.

eISBN: 978-1-68192-604-9
LCCN: 2020935727

Cover design: Tyler Ottinger
Cover photograph: Jamie Dunek
Interior design: Amanda Falk
Interior photos: Photos of the author and his family are provided courtesy of the author.
Mother Teresa photo credit: Paul C. Clerici.

PRINTED IN THE UNITED STATES OF AMERICA

*This book is dedicated to the women who have
impacted my life and in fact saved my life.*

*To our Blessed Mother Mary, for your continued intercession on
my behalf, for the love and mercy you have always shown me.*

*To Saint Mother Teresa, for your "yes" to Our
Lord and to the poor and forgotten. Your kindness
and mercy changed everything for me.*

*To Mother Elvira of Comunita Cenacolo, for your sacrifice,
your service, and your joy. You have been a reflection of
God's love and mercy for me and my family as well as
the thousands of other families you have touched.*

*To my mother, Alma, who suffered greatly as a
result of my addiction, thank you for never giving
up on me and for your endless prayers.*

*To my wife, Benerada, my partner and my best friend. Your
love and support have meant the world to me. Our Lord
picked you to walk on this journey with me, and you have
made me a better man. You are the love of my life. Thank
you for everything you have done for me and our family.*

*To my daughter, Kyra, thank you for being the amazing young
woman of God that you are. You are in my prayers always.*

CONTENTS

FOREWORD

"I give this book my approval." End of story ... isn't that enough? When Jimmy Wahlberg asked me to write something for his book, I thought it would be a small blurb on the back cover. I could do that. I have done it a number of times for some talented authors who wrote incredible books. All of these were books that I believed in, just like I believe in *The Big Hustle*. It was Jimmy's follow-up question that I wasn't sure about: "Will you write the foreword?"

It's not that I didn't want to do it. Rather, I kept putting it off because I wasn't sure that I could do the book, the topic, or, more importantly, Jimmy's mission, justice. To understand this book, you have to understand this one concept right off the bat: This isn't just a story.

I met Jimmy at a boxing match in Las Vegas on May 2,

2015. Alcohol was pretty prevalent, as one might expect from the venue and the city. Jim let me know right from the start that he didn't drink. I liked his candor. Anybody who really knows me knows that I am direct and to the point, so I appreciated that about Jimmy as well. It wasn't too far into the conversation that Jim started to tell me his story, and how his path through addiction had led him to redemption at the foot of the cross. I, too, know that story well. However, it would be another cross in a distant land that would call his oldest son, Daniel.

My path would cross with Daniel later that same summer. It would be about as far away from the likes of Las Vegas as you could get, set in a tiny village in Hercegovina called Medjugorje. Medjugorje is a Croatian village where six children began in 1981 receiving apparitions of the Blessed Virgin Mary, and continued up to 2020. I have visited Medjugorje as a pilgrim over seven times, and I have seen the power of the faith that is present in that community. Millions from around the world flock to Medjugorje to visit "the cross on the hill" for one reason. This village boasts of a peace that is elusive to find and even harder to maintain. It is here that Jimmy's son Daniel came to find peace.

Jim and Daniel are unequivocally and unapologetically Catholic. I respect that about them both, not just because I am Catholic, but because they, like me, realize that it is their faith that gives them unique voices in the battle of addiction and the perseverant strength to overcome. As a father of three, I keep thinking about all of the influences that our children face. As parents, we all wonder and worry: How can we guard our children and keep them safe?

This is why Jimmy Wahlberg's autobiographical account of his life grabbed my attention from the start. Something about this story must be grabbing your attention as well because you are holding it in your hands. Whatever reason you had for picking up this book, do yourself a favor and don't just hold it. Read it all. Yes, it's an incredible story of redemption, and it reads like a come-from-behind, against-all-odds thriller. Even more importantly, you are going to see yourself and your loved ones in these pages.

Maybe you didn't grow up in a poor neighborhood like Jimmy did. Maybe you haven't had issues with substance abuse touch you or your family — at least not yet. Regardless, as you read this story, many elements will touch you personally. They touched me personally. Addiction affects all of us.

This isn't just a story of one man's journey from the hell of addiction to sobriety; it is a wake-up call for every individual, parent, teacher, minister, priest, and bishop to see the mission at hand. God never wants us to experience pain, but sin is pain, and some of our sinful decisions and the decisions of those closest to us lead to pain. The hope is that God, if we allow him, can turn our sin and our pain into a mission of love. If you finish this book and grasp that one essential concept of "a mission of love," I believe this book will have served a great purpose.

Blessings!

James Caviezel

INTRODUCTION
MY SON, THE ADDICT

I'd been in fights all my life. I'd been pummeled by the toughest guys you'd ever *not* want to meet. I'd been beaten up, knocked unconscious, whacked in the head with a crowbar, and thrashed by a prison guard. But far and away the worst gut punch I ever took was when I discovered that my son was on drugs.

Daniel was sixteen years old. His behavior had been off, his energy seemed low, but we attributed that to recently losing his best friend to cancer.

Here I was, working in the field of addiction, a supposed expert, and I didn't see anything at all. I was blind to it. But my wife, Benny, wasn't. She suspected that something was going on. So she got hold of Daniel's phone and looked at his text messages. Many of them were indecipherable, as if written in code. She went out and bought a drug test.

Benny had been through this hell before. Her brother had been addicted to crack and then heroin and was deported back to the Dominican Republic. Her mother hadn't held him accountable; he was always welcomed back to sleep and eat at home. She even did his laundry.

That indulgent, my-kid-can-do-no-wrong approach had failed spectacularly. Benny wasn't going to make the same mistake. When she came home with the drug test, she asked — or told — me to clear everyone out of the house. Now, it happens that Daniel was a very talented music producer, even at that precocious age. He had a studio in our garage, and people paid good money to work with him. That particular day he was in the studio with an All-Pro NFL cornerback. The football star was an aspiring rapper, and Daniel was making music for him to rap to.

I burst into the studio and said: "Sorry, but everybody's got to get out. Right now. We have family business to attend to."

The cornerback was looking at me with one of those "Don't you know who I am?" stares, but I didn't care. I kicked them all out.

My son didn't know what was going on. But he knew it wasn't good.

I brought him upstairs. My wife gave him a cup and told him to pee in it. At that moment I watched Daniel transform into a different person. He looked right into my eyes and lied to me.

It was the typical drug-user BS. "Oh, man, like I tried pot once, a month ago. It was my first time. I didn't like it. I don't do it anymore, but it's probably gonna show up on this test."

I knew the translation: "I smoke weed all day, every day."

It all started to make sense. As a guy who grew up poor, I like to have a lot of cash in my pocket. It gives me a sense of security. I keep it on the nightstand. And for the last year or so there'd been times when the wallet on my nightstand had less money within than it should have had. I figured that perhaps Benny had taken the money, or maybe I'd been hit in the head too many times and was losing my edge. Never in a million years would I have thought my son was stealing from me. (Even though as a boy I had done the exact same thing to my loved ones.)

But as soon as I saw his face when he was asked to pee in that cup, I knew. It all flashed before my eyes. My son was on drugs.

I lost it. I was screaming at him as loud as I could. I'd warned Daniel his entire life that he was descended from a long line of idiots on both sides of his family who had destroyed their lives with alcohol and drugs. With that kind of lineage, you can't gamble with this garbage.

"Why don't you just go jump off the roof," I yelled, "because you're gonna kill yourself!"

Believe me, I knew what I was talking about. Because it's only by the grace of God that I hadn't killed myself with drugs and alcohol long before that day.

CHAPTER ONE
A BAD SEED?

The first place I ever lived was in an upstairs apartment over a bar called the Sands Café at the corner of Park Street and Adams Street in the Fields Corner district of the Boston neighborhood of Dorchester. That's also the neighborhood in which I would meet and fall in love with my wife — but we're getting ahead of ourselves.

I guess it makes sense that I was born over a bar because I spent all of my teenage years and a good part of my young adulthood drunk. My dad worked there — and he drank there, too. There's a family story that when I was maybe one year old, walking but still in diapers, I slipped out of the apartment. My mother couldn't find me anywhere. Then she looked out the window. There was a bowling alley across the street, with kids and derelicts hanging out in front. And there I was, hanging out with them, a derelict in training, amusing the older kids with my minuscule vocabulary, in which the f-word was featured right alongside *Mama* and *Dada*.

From the very beginning, I was looking for acceptance. Trying to impress the older kids. Just wanting to be cool and to be appreciated and to be loved. And looking for all this, as the song goes, in the wrong places.

As far back as I can remember, I was always into something. In kindergarten I stole the milk money from my school-teacher. Seriously, I did. Then I pulled a similar stunt in the second grade. I had a classmate, John Paul, who looked much older than me, but we were in the same grade. He and I stole the milk money from the teacher's desk. We hid it. I went back and stole it again. John Paul found out and beat me up.

It felt like someone was always looking for me. Someone was always accusing me of doing something. And I was always worried about getting caught. There was just no peace in my head or in my life. It was a constant state of unease. And I was all of seven years old.

• • •

Dorchester in the 1970s, when I came of age, was a working-class neighborhood, one of the poorer sections of Boston, and very racially segregated. It was mostly Catholic, and most of those Catholics were Irish. Relatively healthy parishes and a sense of social solidarity held it all together.

Dorchester is part of Boston. We're served by the Boston Police Department and Boston Public Schools. We pull for the Red Sox, the Patriots, the Celtics, and the Bruins. But Boston is, or it certainly was when I was growing up, a city of neighbor-hoods: Southie, Charlestown, Jamaica Plain, Roxbury … and Dorchester.

Dorchester was overwhelmingly Irish. Yeah, my last name is Walhberg, which isn't exactly O'Leary or Flaherty, but my mom, Alma, is Irish (maiden name Donnelly) and my father, Donald, was an unusual blend of Irish and Swedish. His father, my grandfather, was a first-generation Swede named Axel Si-mon Wahlberg, and he married an Irish woman named Mary Madeline Bradley.

I do have a distinguished connection, though, to the old WASP New England. Through my mom I am the fourth cous-in, eight times removed, of the nineteenth-century novelist Nathaniel Hawthorne, who wrote *The Scarlet Letter* and other works about sin and guilt. Cousin Nathaniel could have found a lot to write about in my life, for sure.

• • •

I was the middle kid, fifth in a lineup of nine. We could have fielded our own baseball team. I had eight brothers and sisters. In order of age, we are Debbie (the first of my siblings to pass), Michelle (who died in December 2019), Arthur, Paul, me, Trac-ey, Bob, Donnie, and Mark. You've probably heard of my two youngest brothers.

I was starved for attention. We all were.

Eleven of us plus our dog were living at 128 Buttonwood Street in a three-bedroom apartment on the second floor of a three-decker house. We were poor and crammed in on top of each other, but so was everyone else in the neighborhood, and I felt fine living there.

If you needed something, you could call on your neighbor and they would give it to you. Everybody had permission to kick your kid's butt if he was doing something wrong. The whole "it takes a village to raise a child" idea has become distorted into a cliché, but in close-knit neighborhoods it really is true. I can't help but idealize those early years. It seemed as if Buttonwood were one big happy family. The street used to flood like crazy. I remember once we swam in the puddles.

Despite my chronic misbehavior, that time was the one happy interlude in my childhood. It ended when I was eight years old.

Then my father hit a number with this bookie who did business out of his car parked on Mount Vernon Street. A mobile office, you might call it. I'm not sure how big a haul my father got, but it was enough, at the very least, for him to make a down payment on a house that cost about $20,000 in 1973. I'm guessing the payoff was somewhere in the area of five grand.

So we moved into a nice house on Mercier Avenue, a decent little middle-class neighborhood. And I became aware, for the first time, of all the things we *didn't* have.

There we were, a double-digit family living on Mercier Avenue because my father hit a number with a bookie, and we were trying to keep up with the Joneses and failing. The Joneses had two kids and two cars. We had nine kids, usually no car, and a dog. Our washer and dryer were constantly breaking down from overuse, so we'd fill garbage bags with our dirty laundry and walk down the street looking like homeless urchins carrying those garbage bags to the bus to go to the laundromat. We were a spectacle, and we were ashamed.

Or we'd be sent to the corner grocery store with our food stamps and be too embarrassed to use them if anyone we knew happened to be in the store. My brother Paul's buddies worked there, and I'd wait for as long as it took for them to go on break or punch out for the day so I could use the food stamps with the Greek or Asian owner working at the cash register — someone I didn't know and who didn't know my family. (Oddly, I was never embarrassed to *steal* my parents' food stamps and use them on the way to school to buy candy bars and junk food.)

I always had the feeling that our neighbors were looking down on us: this big unruly brood with my father's delivery truck parked out front. I never brought friends to my house. I was too embarrassed by our strained circumstances. Plus, my father drank, and you never knew what kind of mood he might be in. Add to that the fact that I was always in trouble, so I might come home to learn that my parents found out something I did that I didn't even know I'd been caught for yet.

I thought the people who had the things we didn't have were somehow better than us. What a warped perspective that was — as if our possessions define us. But that's what I thought.

• • •

We were raised without a strong religious faith. Yes, we were technically Catholic, but this really was just a case of checking off boxes, or submitting to ceremonies or declarations of faith in a rote and passionless way.

I'm saddened by this. I have felt keenly the absence of faith, but I can't say that I resent my parents for their failure to bring us up in a strong and meaningful Catholic tradition. They just weren't capable of it.

You can't transmit something you don't have.

You see, they never received this gift from their own parents. Both my father and mother grew up in major dysfunction. Their households had very little love.

I remember talking to my Uncle Archie once about his upbringing. He's my dad's brother — ninety-three at this writing — and a great guy. He wanted to have a better understanding of my relationship with my father.

I told him that I'd never heard my dad say, "I love you," except perhaps when he'd had a few drinks in him.

"Consider yourself lucky," my uncle said. "Because we never heard it at all."

This helped me look at my dad in a different, more understanding light. He'd had a difficult life. He was ill-equipped to serve as father of nine kids.

He didn't know how to, and didn't have the time to, perform even the most basic fatherly functions. For instance, I never once played catch with my father. Not once. I do, however, remember him on one occasion making an effort to spend quality time with me. I was in elementary school. The red lights and warning signs that I was perhaps a bit crazy were already blinking like mad. So one day my father came to school early and took me out to go to the movies.

Our cinematic father-son fare for the day? A double feature of Clint Eastwood's *Dirty Harry* and *Magnum Force*. Good movies, for sure. But R-rated movies — definitely not suitable for the under-ten set. Yet it was a moment that we shared, just the two of us, and however inappropriate the movies may have been, it was special for me.

He meant well. He wanted to spend some quality time with his mixed-up kid. But it was a miscalculation, to put it mildly. And that's the only thing I ever remember us doing together, just us.

Another memory. My dad built a picket fence that went all around the wooden house at 60 Mercier Avenue. A very front-porch, Middle American thing to do. He had some of us kids paint it white — just like Tom Sawyer and Huck Finn!

I was painting away, enjoying myself. I was doing my best, but I was no pro. I was a nine- or ten-year-old kid painting a fence. My dad looked at my work and said, in a strongly disapproving voice, "What good is it if you paint it if I have to paint it again?"

Here I am now, fifty-four years old, and I've never forgotten that. Those words stung. I'm sure he wasn't intending any lasting harm by it. He didn't want to scar me for life or anything like that. Heck, he probably forgot it ten seconds after he said it — but it's one of those hurts that never went away. An indelible memory, and a bad one. The message I got was that I wasn't good enough.

I believe that it's far less likely — not impossible, but far less likely — that a man of God would speak to his son or daughter like that. I spend a lot of time talking to parents these days about addiction and how it relates to brokenness. A lot of times we can determine what causes someone's brokenness. It can be one big thing, or it can be an accumulation of things, including hurtful or hateful remarks. We all have different levels of sensitivity. You can call me a baldheaded so-and-so and it bounces right off me, whereas it might really wound another man. This is especially true of kids. But my dad just lacked an awareness of this pretty basic fact.

Hey, he had nine kids. Nine mouths to feed. You can't spend all your time lavishing individual attention on each one of them. You have to keep clothes on their backs, make sure the bills are paid. And when you're raised by people who never expressed love to you, an awareness of potential slights is hopelessly distant from your mind.

My uncle said that there was just no kindness in their house. No gentleness. His mom — my paternal grandmother — was a tough lady. She was not a nice person. Certainly not the kind of grandmother who smothered her grandkids with love and affection.

I spent some time with her as a child. She was never mean to us. Rigid, but not mean. In fact, it used to be a treat to spend a night or a weekend at her house. She was a widow who lived by herself, or sometimes she lived with my dad's other brother, my Uncle Paul Wahlberg, who was my godfather. Her cupboards were full of Oreos and other snacks that we seldom had at our house. But the cookies weren't free; you had to pay the price. It might mean shoveling snow or helping with other household chores. If you were really unlucky, it meant rubbing lotion on her crusty old feet. Just what every nine-year-old wants to do!

But I was willing to pay that price because it removed me, if only for a day or a weekend, from the insanity of our house. I could even sleep in a bed all by myself! (At home we slept two to a bunk bed. Two up. Two down. One person's head at the headboard, the other's at the baseboard, so that you usually woke up with someone's feet in your face. Though at least you didn't have to rub lotion on them.)

My mother, too, grew up in a dysfunctional family of alcoholics, though she was always a hugger, a kisser, a woman who knew how to say, and who frequently said, "I love you."

Mom was a people pleaser. In our house she was always trying to keep the peace, and to keep the yelling to a minimum. That's how she'd grown up: trying to keep her mom and dad from fighting with each other, and to keep her sisters from getting in trouble.

My mother tells a heartbreaking story about when she was a little girl. One year all the presents under the Christmas tree were from her to her family. There were no other presents. She was just a kid, and she took it upon herself to make Christmas special for the others — even if the others did not reciprocate. She says that the smiles on the faces of her family were her gift. It's a beautiful story, but it's sad: a little eight-year-old girl struggling to hold her dysfunctional family together, to make it normal. Trying to make the members of her family love one another — something they were incapable of doing.

I have to say, that's one thing my parents did really well. We had nothing, but on Christmas they would go crazy. One year we all got bicycles. Yes, nine new bicycles purchased with the modest wages of a delivery truck driver and a night-shift worker. My father probably hit a number or borrowed the money from a loan shark to get those bicycles. Or else he went even deeper into debt. But whatever it took, there were always presents at Christmas.

• • •

Booze is a tyrant in the family of an alcoholic. It shapes and distorts every relationship. But I don't want to give the impression that it was the be-all and end-all of my father's existence. Far from it. He was an excellent cook, a talent my brother Paul has inherited and expanded upon. Dad also had a creative, even artistic streak. He had a talent for drawing, and when he was young he took sign-painting classes. I've wondered if he ever had dreams or ambitions in that direction. Maybe he did.

But he had no time for dreams.

Not only were there nine of us kids at home, but my father also had three kids from a previous marriage. This was never discussed in our house, at least not within my earshot. I never even knew these step-siblings existed until I was an adult.

One of my stepbrothers — an alcoholic, not surprisingly, for he had suffered from his own demons — reached out to us after he achieved sobriety. He wanted to know this other part of his family. He contacted my brother Bob, who hosted a gathering at which we all met. Another stepbrother was also an alcoholic, and the third sibling, a sister, wanted nothing to do with us. Not everyone likes to meet new brothers and sisters in middle age.

My uncle told me that my dad's first wife left him for another man. She had slandered him up one side and down the other, claiming that he was abusive. My uncle said it was all lies. She was just trading in my father for an upgrade. She left him for the neighborhood bookie, who had a pocketful of money, which was all her heart desired.

But there's one really outstanding thing my father did, and he deserves great credit for this act. He took on an instant family when he married my mother. She'd had three kids — Debbie, Michelle, and Arthur — with this guy with whom she lived. They broke up because he was an alcoholic … and then Alma Elaine Donnelly married Donald Wahlberg, who was also an alcoholic.

But my father showed some real character. He raised those kids as if they were his own flesh and blood. I never once heard him use the words *adopted* or *stepbrother* or *stepsister*. They were his children and my brothers and sisters — period. That was a standup thing for him to do.

• • •

I had my first drink when I was eight years old. By "first drink" I don't mean I had a sip of Communion wine at church, or that my father let me take a swallow or two from his bottle of beer.

No, I was tagging along with some older boys, who thought it was funny to watch a little kid chug beer. Nothing really happened. I didn't get caught. I didn't get in trouble. I remember an overwhelming feeling of acceptance from the older kids. I liked that. I felt like I belonged.

The next time I drank, I was nine years old, hanging around the Woodrow Wilson schoolyard on a summer weekend afternoon. It was a similar situation. There were older kids, maybe fifteen or sixteen years old, and I wanted to impress them. I had stolen someone's wallet out of a locker at the Dorchester YMCA. It had $50 in it, which I brought to Brad, a hippie kid who lived close to the school. For fifty bucks Brad gave me a quart of Budweiser and a pack of Marlboros. Some deal, eh? In 1974 they cost maybe a dollar combined.

I drank the quart of Bud while sitting on the steps behind the school.

Then the party moved around the corner to a grassy hill. I'd finished my Budweiser, but I couldn't seem to get enough. So I started grabbing other people's beers and drinking them.

Finally, I went home. I walked down to the playroom in the basement, where we had a TV and a broken ping-pong table. Actually, we had two TVs stacked one upon the other. On the bottom was a color TV with a picture but no sound, and on top was a black and white TV with sound but no picture. They complemented each other beautifully.

I was watching *Creature Double Feature*, and the room

started spinning. I staggered up the stairs and into the kitchen, hoping to make it outside. I didn't make it.

My mother had a perch at the kitchen counter where she'd sit in her chair and smoke cigarettes and talk on the phone. I tripped over the kitchen threshold and threw up all over the kitchen floor. "What's that smell?" she asked my sister as I knelt in vomit. "Smell it!" Obviously it was booze.

"Are you crazy?" screamed my mother. "You're nine years old!" She asked where I got the beer. I ratted out the older kids. So Mom marched over to Brad's house, took off her shoe, and beat him over the head with it.

At home, my old man spanked me and grounded me. I guess that grounding was my first sentence. The next morning, when I came down to breakfast, he gave me a whack. I wish it had hurt enough to have deterred me from the road I was about to follow. But it didn't even come close. He was really peeved for three or four days. After they cooled off a bit, my parents lectured me. They told me I was just a kid and I should just go be a little kid instead of a budding juvenile delinquent. I didn't give the idea a second thought.

When they told me that my punishment was lifted and that I could go outside and play, I ran out the door of my house and within five minutes I was back at Brad's house, ready to pay the penalty for snitching on him as long as I could have more beer.

Some major transformation had already occurred inside me. I just wanted to be with these kids, to do what they were doing, to be accepted. I wanted to be loved and wanted. I felt invisible in my own home, with nine kids and my parents working all the time to put food on the table. I thought I'd fallen through the cracks and landed with these teenagers.

Brad didn't beat me up for snitching. But I paid a price.

I became the group's gofer. They'd tell me to steal ten bucks from my father, and I'd do it. After a moving truck unloaded a new family's boxes and possessions into the house next door to Brad's, the other kids opened a window, threw me in, and had me open the door for them. They robbed the people blind. It never occurred to me that this was wrong.

• • •

If you were a neighbor of ours on Mercier Avenue, you might look out the window on Sunday morning and see a line of Wahlberg kids, dressed in what passed for our Sunday best, leaving the house and walking, presumably, to church. What a cute sight! What a sweet Catholic family!

Not quite. Because while we all left the house with the ostensible destination of St. Gregory's Church, that's not where we were going to end up. You see, my parents didn't accompany us; they just whisked us out the door.

We did set foot in church — barely. We would all walk in, everybody would grab a bulletin to prove we'd been there, and then we'd dart out, typically to Walsh Park, where we'd sit on a hill and watch the cops play softball in their Sunday morning league.

Vendors would be selling the Sunday Boston papers outside the church. When Mass started, some vendors would go in, and others would gather in one spot to chat. People who came when no one was manning the fort would take a paper and leave their money under a rock. Well, it didn't take me long to figure out that this was like an open invitation to steal. So I'd wait till no one was around, take the money from underneath the rock, and scram.

On rare occasions I would actually sit through a Mass, sometimes with my mother. When I did go to church, I always had the feeling that the people there thought they were better than me. Or that they were staring at me or judging me. Looking back as an adult, I can see that this was nonsense. It was my misperception; it had nothing to do with their behavior. They were living their own lives, praying and raising children and trying to have a relationship with Christ. They weren't thinking about me. They didn't care about me.

We went through the motions of being Catholic, but there was no substance to it. I made my first Communion (though not my confirmation), but it was just checking something off a list. It was what everyone else was doing. It was a reason to dress up in a white suit, a reason to have a little gathering, a reason for people to give you envelopes with a few bucks inside, but it wasn't about having a relationship with God. It had nothing to do with faith. It was just tradition … something you were supposed to do for some inscrutable and long-forgotten reason.

Nobody in my home taught me about a loving God. Nobody ever opened a Bible. Nobody taught me about Jesus Christ.

So I never felt part of a faith community. I never felt under the eye of a loving God. All I remember hearing of God is that God is gonna get you if you don't watch out. God's watching — and he's just waiting for you to make a mistake. He was a God of vengeance and punishment, not mercy and love.

What a terrible thing to do to a kid. To threaten a kid with God. To completely miss out on the opportunity to explain to a child that we are all sinners, we are all flawed, we are all going to make mistakes, but nevertheless God loves us and will forgive us if we come to him and ask for that forgiveness.

No one explained to me that we are members of a living

faith, and that we know that there is something after this — and that all of us, down to the lowliest child, can be part of it. What I wouldn't have given to have learned these truths. But no one ever explained them to me. So I'd be in church, looking around, feeling disconnected, certain that I didn't belong there — that I wasn't even worthy of being there.

That was a common theme throughout my life: a kind of self-loathing, or a lack of self-love. That happens when you start to ingest alcohol and drugs at a very young age. You're doing things that cause people to look at you a certain way, and you develop the sense that you're always being watched, being judged, and not favorably.

In my case, if something went missing, I was always blamed — even if I had nothing to do with it. I was just presumed guilty. Everyone thought I did it. I had a track record, to be sure; I can't really blame people for jumping to the conclusion that I was the guilty party. But it does something to a kid.

Like shortly before we moved from Buttonwood Street, my mother's welfare check came up missing. Everybody figured I'd stolen it. I hadn't. But by the time we moved to the house on Mercier, I had heard so many times that I'd swiped this check that I weaved a story to Brad and the guys about my daring theft: how I'd hidden it in a secret place and was waiting for the right moment to retrieve it. All fantasy.

Heck, I even got blamed once for burning down a school — and believe it or not, I did not do it.

I was in third grade at the Gilbert Stuart Elementary School on Richmond Street in Dorchester. The date was April 22, 1974. I was locked in my upstairs room at home, being punished for some transgression or other. The school caught fire and burned to the ground — and I got accused of the crime!

The teachers thought I did it. The Boston public school bureaucracy thought I did it. Even my mother, the person who had sent me to my room, thought I did it. It's as if I started the fire by pyrokinesis!

With Gilbert Stuart out of commission, I was transferred to Charles Taylor School, which is right across the street from the Mattapan projects. It was the borderline between black and white Dorchester.

Since they were convinced that I had burned down Gilbert Stuart, they put my desk next to the principal's office at Charles Taylor for the remainder of the school year. Look, I was a bad seed. I wasn't like the painter Gilbert Stuart's most famous subject, George Washington, who supposedly said as a boy, "I cannot tell a lie." But I'm telling the God's honest truth when I say that I did not set fire to Gilbert Stuart Elementary.

In fourth grade I went to Joseph E. Lee School, and in fifth to William Monroe Trotter School on Humboldt Avenue in Dorchester, right on the border of Roxbury, Boston's most famous black neighborhood. For one year, in sixth grade, I attended my neighborhood school, Woodrow Wilson, but in seventh grade I was shipped to Martin Luther King.

I went to seven different schools from grade one to grade seven, which was my last year of formal public education. So I was the new kid every year. It's not because we moved around all the time. The reason for this different-school-every-year odyssey was that I grew up during the infamous period of busing in Boston — the court-ordered integration of Boston public schools.

Black kids were being bused to mostly white schools, white kids were being bused to mostly black schools, the whole idea of neighborhood schools was in eclipse, and shootings and stabbings and mini-riots were rampant.

The morning bus ride might take half an hour to forty-five minutes, sometimes longer when the driver had to alter the route to avoid the threat of violence. Buses were frequently escorted by the police. At that point in the 1970s, the nation was also facing gas shortages. There were long lines at gas stations, but somehow there was always enough gasoline to fuel the buses that ran in and out of Dorchester as part of the court-ordered integration of the public schools. Children were being used as pawns by both sides. The courts packed them on buses and sent them on long rides, far from their neighborhoods; and then some parents and agitators screamed and yelled hateful racial epithets at the little black boys and girls who were coming on buses from the other direction. It was horrific. And we were in the middle of it all.

So I was living with chaos not only within our home but even on the bus ride to school. In retrospect it seems incredible. Seven different schools in seven years? That's unheard of, unless you're a military brat. And there's significant literature that being constantly uprooted in childhood can have serious psychological effects on people, making it harder to establish connections, put down roots, or regard anything or anybody as permanent.

The images I carry from those years aren't of readin' and writin' and 'rithmetic in a little red schoolhouse where kids bring apples to the teacher and we all cheer on the good old alma mater. When I think of my schooling in the mid-1970s in Boston, I see grown men and women standing outside schools yelling threats at children. Adults are throwing bottles and rocks, and there are chains and police dogs and cops trying to keep order with nightsticks, and everybody's mad at everybody else. I saw it on the streets in the daytime and on the news at night. Some of these people actually wanted to hurt innocent little children.

We were just a bunch of poor people at one another's throats. And the politicians and judges who set this all in motion, who set us against one another, were rich people who sent their kids to exclusive private schools and whose families didn't have to pay any price or bear any burden for their acts.

I used to wonder why we, the poor whites and blacks, didn't work together. We had a lot more in common than we had separating us. But nobody was listening to a nine-year-old. Boston — not the rich areas, but certainly the working-class and poor sections, especially Southie, Charlestown, and Dorchester — was a powder keg of racial hostility.

Except at our house. My mother was very liberal when it came to race relations. We had black friends over to the house all the time. I remember coming home one day and telling her that I got into a fight with a black kid.

"And why does the color of his skin matter?" she said. "You got in a fight at school. That's all that matters to me."

I came to learn that she was right. The issue wasn't race; it was poverty. The whites of Dorchester were poor. The blacks of Roxbury were poor. And both sides were manipulated into thinking that the other was the enemy, when in reality we had more in common with each other than we did with the rich people who were making the rules.

In this respect as well as many others, my father wasn't like my mother. It's not that he was out there protesting or throwing eggs at little kids. But he was mad, as most of our neighbors were. He didn't think it was right. I don't think it was the right policy, either. There's a value to neighborhood schools, to being able to walk to school in a familiar setting. But the schools in the poorer neighborhoods, especially the black neighborhoods, were being shortchanged. They deserved more resources, a fairer shake.

When I was being bused as a fourth-grader to Joseph E. Lee School in Dorchester, a PBS crew came to our classroom. They did a story on the contrast between the ugliness out on the streets, where adults were venting rage and resentment and hostility, and the relative calm inside the school, where kids of different colors were becoming friends. A big part of the story featured me and two friends, one black and one Spanish-speaking. We were running around the schoolyard playing kickball and laughing and being blissfully oblivious to the fear and hatred on the outside.

• • •

It may sound like I was an absolute terror, more evil than impish, but there were two versions of me.

Coexisting uneasily with the thief and the ten-year-old drunkard was an ordinary kid who hung out with the other kids in our neighborhood, running around and climbing on garage roofs and playing *SWAT* while we hummed its theme song. I had a friend named Lorenzo, a first-generation Italian American whose dad grew grapes in their backyard and made wine in their basement. They had a blackberry tree whose branches extended over their garage. I'd climb up and pick the berries and just lie there on the garage roof eating those blackberries. It's an idyllic kid's memory that comes back to me whenever I eat a blackberry today.

Yet the other side of me was drawn to the streets from a ridiculously young age. My friends and I would hang out around Woodrow Wilson School down Mercier Avenue, which I attended in the sixth grade. (My mother had gone there as well; our roots run pretty deep.) Sometimes I'd just be playing football or baseball on our makeshift playground, but inevitably I'd be drawn to less wholesome activities.

I remember when I was ten years old, I stole weed out of my oldest sister Debbie's pocketbook. I hid it in a cigarette pack. I was sitting on the steps of Woodrow Wilson playing poker with a friend. (Poker was the Wahlberg family game.) Each of us had a pack of cigarettes. My father walked by on the way to the liquor store. He saw the cigarettes. "Whose are those?" he said. "Oh, man," I thought, "I'm busted." Then he slapped me in front of my friend.

I was so embarrassed. I jumped up and screamed, "I effing hate you!" (except I didn't say "effing") and ran off in the other direction. I wish I could say that this exchange was out of character for both of us.

The liquor store my father was headed to is where he played his numbers. He played every day. Sometimes he'd send me as his errand boy. He'd hand me a note and a five-dollar bill, and I'd trot over to pick up his Winstons, his Schlitz, and his numbers. I don't suppose they sell beer and cigarettes to ten-year-old kids anymore, but those were different times. Now and then I'd keep the money intended for his numbers, and if he hit a winner that day and I hadn't put the number in, he'd want to kill me.

• • •

I practically lived at the Dorchester YMCA, playing floor hockey and basketball and swimming, and smoking weed and playing poker and stealing. I was just always drawn to the kids who were getting in trouble — the bad element. But there was a good element at the Y, too, and a family feeling, though for me at that time that was a mixed blessing.

You see, I stole from people's lockers. I even stole from the little box on the front desk which contained the fees from those who used the swimming pool. But in a weird way I stole from the Y because it meant so much to me. It was like family, and I didn't feel worthy of their love. That's messed up, I know. But I was about as messed up a kid as you'll ever find.

I was a good swimmer and might have done something with that if I hadn't cared only about getting drunk and high. When I was eleven or twelve, I won a scholarship to a summer diving program at Boston University, organized and taught by Cal Locke, who had been a great NCAA diver at SMU. Locke had scouted the YMCAs and Boys Clubs of the Boston area and invited what he thought were the best prospects to learn diving under his tutelage.

It was a great opportunity, but I smoked weed all the way to BU and all the way home. So did the kids I traveled with. I took a dive, all right, but it wasn't into an Olympic-sized pool.

Nevertheless, sports played a big role in my family's life. We loved all the Boston teams. I remember watching Carlton Fisk of the Red Sox hit his famous foul-pole hugging home run against the Cincinnati Reds in the 1975 World Series with my whole family yelling and screaming. Well, not quite my whole family — my dad was asleep. It was late, and he had to be to work at 4:00 a.m.

I played all the sports — baseball, basketball, football, street hockey — but usually of the sandlot or pickup variety. The only organized sport I played was Little League baseball. I was a pitcher for a local team called the Angels. When I stood on that mound warming up, every pitch was a strike right down the pipe. But as soon as a batter stepped into the box, I was wild. I must have set a beanball record.

The expensive sports like ice hockey were out. Skates, pads, sticks, and ice time were prohibitively expensive. We couldn't afford that. In fact, anything enjoyable that I did that normal kids also did came as part of an organized activity: trips to the beach, trips to the amusement park, even summer camp. I cried all the way to camp the one year I went, and then I cried all the way home because I didn't want to leave.

My family relied a good deal on the kindness of strangers. And people were kind, whether at the Y, the Boys Club, or even teachers at school. Mrs. Oberg, my sixth-grade music teacher, used to take a student home every week for dinner. Her husband would cook, and the Obergs and the students would just hang out, talking and learning about each other. No way you could do that now. Too much bad stuff has happened, and there's a strain of paranoia in the air, too: people are suspicious. But I loved Mrs. Oberg, who was young and passionate about her calling as a teacher. I loved music then and now, and I still remember the songs she taught us. She saw that passion in me, and she saw past my troublemaking, my hardness, and the fact that in other classes I was not paying attention and was a holy terror.

Mrs. Oberg, if you're out there reading this: Thank you.

• • •

My first best friend after we moved to Mercier Avenue was a guy named John. Soon enough I started hanging with John's younger brother Paul. Their dad was a bus driver and an alcoholic, and their household was as chaotic as the rest. Paul was violent. He'd been bullied mercilessly as a little kid, but then he shot up overnight and went from getting pushed around to knocking people out. I had to be on my toes around him. I'd teased him back when he was a sad sack, and I knew he was a time bomb of anger and resentment.

These early friends formed the nucleus of the Ashmont Station gang. We weren't a gang in any organized sense of the word, but we partied together all the time, drinking and smoking weed and playing poker, and sometimes playing pickup sports games, too. Most of 'em were older than me. I was the only twelve-year-old in town who drew his self-esteem (or what passed for self-esteem) from hanging out with sixteen-year-olds. I would do anything to impress them. If they said, "Here's a bat. Go hit that guy and we'll love you," I was the man to do it.

It was me and Sean and Michael and Greg and Steve and Paul and Gerard, who went on to become, in no particular order, a Marine, a coke dealer, and a prison inmate. Gerard was the toughest guy I've ever met, but he had one weakness: he was addicted to money. We used to joke that he still had the first dollar he ever stole.

We were brought together by our brokenness. That was the common thread of the Ashmont Station gang. But we had other threads in common, too — namely, the designer jeans and polo shirts with upturned collars which we wore in a vain attempt to look fancy.

Driving through that neighborhood today, it seems like every other house carries a set of memories and associations — and most of them involve underage drinking and hell-raising. The VFW Post on Bailey Street … the little schoolhouse … the alley behind the red brick building … all soaked in alcohol in my memory. We didn't drink inside the VFW, of course, but those guys — many of them Vietnam vets, just broken and floundering — were people we looked up to. We aspired to be like them. Not doctors or lawyers or architects or firemen, but drunks. Those were our role models.

Our fathers were almost all alcoholics. Unlike so many broken homes today, most of the dads were in the picture, or at least they were until they weren't. The mothers would kick them out, or they'd leave of their own volition, staggering their way toward their own private hells.

Today, Dorchester is a hot real estate market. People with money are buying up the old homes and renovating them. Parts of it are considered trendy, almost tony. You walk down Ashmont Street and hear a regular Babel of voices — Vietnamese, Cambodian, Jamaican, and, of course, Boston Irish. The people from Vietnam and Cambodia began arriving in the mid- and late '70s, refugees from the Vietnam War.

I came of age, and did a lot damage, on those streets in the 1970s. My world was contained within an obtuse triangle. Ashmont Station, the local train station, was at one point of the triangle, and we considered it our domain. Today it's fancy; back then it was dingy, dirty, kinda seedy. The other two points of the triangle were Ashmont Street and Dorchester Street. We prowled that block like it was ours.

I hung out a lot in front of O'Brien's liquor store, my home away from home. They wouldn't sell me booze. In fact, O'Brien's was just one of the many places from which I was banned. But if certain people were working the register, I could buy a pack of gum.

O'Brien's is still there. So is Johnny's Pizza. Johnny would kick us out now and then, but we'd always come back. That shop was the source of all my nutrition: pizza and ham and cheese subs. Though if I had to choose between a sub and a drink, I'd take the drink. Not that I could walk into the nearby Tara Room and belly up to the bar — I was only twelve or thirteen — but we'd finagle or bribe some adult to buy us a six-pack.

We weren't old enough to drink in the Tara Room, which is now a beauty shop, but we were in and out all the time, selling drugs, looking for potential victims. I was banned for life, but — and this sure would have surprised the bartenders — I outlived the place. The Tara Room, the Irish bar where I would have my first "legal" drink (as if that meant anything to me at the time), is gone with the wind.

We started out selling grass, and when cocaine became more of a street drug, no longer just for the rich, we diversified. We sold, we used, we were under the influence pretty close to twenty-four hours a day. There was nothing glamorous or cool about it; we were lost boys.

We were also constantly in fights. Sometimes these were racially motivated, sometimes not. I was drunk and high all the time. I was either acting like an idiot or trying to get high so I could act like an idiot.

I started hanging out down there around the sixth grade. My first Ashmont friend was Mike, a schoolmate of mine, who lived with his mom and his older brother, Mark. (As I said, most of us — almost all of us — were from homes where dad was either long gone or a drunk.) Mike's mother was a divorced single mom and a wonderful woman. She took in her sister, who had fled a bad marriage in New York, and her three kids.

Mike's cousin Sean and I really connected. We were two broken kids, raised in chaos. I was already getting in trouble constantly: skipping school, stealing money from my parents, or stealing the family's food stamps to buy junk food at the corner store. A whole group of guys coalesced around us, but Sean and I were the ringleaders. Or at least we were the heaviest drinkers and most frequent fighters. Trouble followed us everywhere — but we invited it.

In sixth grade, at the age of eleven, I had my first serious brush with the law. Sean and I were hanging out on Lonsdale Street in Dorchester. Sean had a Swiss army knife. It wasn't a switchblade or anything like that, but we got into an altercation with this guy, and Sean grabbed for the knife. He cut the guy's hand on the blade. We were placed under arrest for assault and battery.

Sean and I went to court together. My mom and dad were there, too. They were angry and frustrated with me, and none too happy that Dad had to take a day off from work to go to court. The judge called Sean and me into his chambers, accompanied by my parents. He had determined to send Sean to juvenile detention and send me home. I looked at my father and thought, "Man, I'd rather go to jail than go home with him." So when the judge sentenced Sean to juvenile detention, I piped up, "You can take me, too."

My father gave me a look that said, "I'm gonna kill you."

The judge said, "Oh, don't worry, when he gets out, I'm sending you." And it wasn't long before I was in trouble again. I would be in and out of detention centers, foster homes, and finally prison for the next fourteen years.

CHAPTER TWO
CHILDHOOD'S END

A writer once called home a "haven in a heartless world," but for me it was a place to flee. I started running away from home when I was nine years old. The first time I lit out was shortly after we moved from Buttonwood to Mercier. Now, it's maybe five miles at the most between those two streets, but to a kid it seemed like one hundred miles. We'd just moved from what would be the only childhood home in which I ever felt safe and protected and loved, and I just didn't want to be in this new house anymore. So I walked back to the old neighborhood. It took me a long time, but it was daylight, and I wasn't scared.

My family knew that I'd run away. They were looking for me. I saw my grandfather's car driving down the street with my mother and grandmother and others packed in. I hid. They passed me by. Once they were out of sight, I started walking again. Then I saw my father's delivery van coming for me. He pulled over. It wasn't some emotional scene in which he cried, "Son," and opened his arms, and I fell into them sobbing as he reassured me of his love. It was more like he wanted to strangle me. When my mom turned the car around and joined us, she was emotional, crying and all.

Little did she know that this would be the first of many, many such unexpected departures — very few of which ended this satisfactorily.

• • •

I only went to my real neighborhood school, Woodrow Wilson, for the sixth grade. I didn't want to go back for a second year. It was too close for comfort. If I played hooky in order to smoke weed, which I did all the time, the principal could just walk down to my house looking for me. That was the downside of proximity to home. I guess it was also the upside of busing.

My last school, my seventh-grade school, was Martin Luther King. It was not where the rich people sent their children.

Martin Luther King is just one block over from Intervale, one of the most dangerous streets in the city. The street is notorious. In 1995, members of the Intervale gang ambushed and killed an assistant state attorney general who was prosecuting some of their associates.

So the last public school I ever attended in Boston was just around the corner from what may be the worst street in the city. But I was only robbed once. A couple of us had climbed out a window, and we were smoking weed on the front steps. This much older, much bigger black kid relieved us of our illicit smokes.

The rule in my house was if you go out, you'd better be home when the streetlights turn on. That was a generational thing, I guess. Nothing good happens to kids once those streetlights flash on. Anyway, it was June, the first Friday night after the seventh grade, and I was drinking with my friends on Ashmont Street. I saw the streetlights flicker on, and I thought to myself, "Uh-oh, I'm not going to make it." So I said the hell with it. I'm not going home. And me being me, I didn't go home until August. I turned thirteen on the streets.

Some people in Massachusetts summer on Cape Cod or Martha's Vineyard; I spent that summer on a porch behind O'Brien's liquor store at the corner of Dorchester Avenue and Ashmont Street. Actually, "porch" is too grand a word. It was basically a wooden box on the second floor with a lounge chair in which I slept.

I drank and got high every day. Sometimes I would see my brothers and sisters around the neighborhood. I must have seemed like a lost sheep to them. Although I tried to act tough, not showing any emotions or vulnerability, I was ashamed, embarrassed by what I'd become and how grim and dismal my future looked to be. They'd written me off; I know they had.

I would see my mom, too. I'd be out by myself late at night, nowhere to go, and I'd see her walking to Ashmont Station to catch a train. She worked overnight in a bank in downtown Boston cleaning the floors and the offices to provide for her family. It was scary for anyone to ride that train at eleven at night, much less a mother of nine. I'd watch her from a distance. I wanted to go to her and say, "Mom, I love you. Please help me." But I didn't. And what could she do? My dad wasn't going to let me back. And Mom had to go to work. There were still eight kids to feed at home.

Even today, when I think about my past sorrows, that image comes back to me. I knew I was breaking her heart. I knew I made her already difficult life more difficult. Actually, I did approach her one time. I followed her to the train station at a distance, and then I closed that distance. I just said, "Mom." She looked at me with the saddest eyes. I could see behind them the question, "How did your young life come to this?"

I didn't know the answer. Neither did she. She got on the train. I watched it pull away.

My father was running the show, so she couldn't tell me to come home even if she'd wanted to. I used to think, "I'll never treat my kids like this." Only as an adult did I realize that my dad came from a generation in which thirteen-year-olds like him had jobs. He quit school to help provide for his family. I'm sure if he had behaved like I did, his father would have booted him out of the house, too. But still, it hurt.

The older I got the more emotional the memory became of my mother walking to the train station in the dark of night on her way to scrub floors, on her hands and knees, to feed the family. As both a son and a father, this breaks my heart. I regret what a rotten child I was. At the time I thought: "Oh, they have eight other kids to worry about. They don't care about me." Of course, they *did* care about me — no matter how lost I was.

It hurts me today to think how much I hurt her back then. As much as I told myself that she didn't care, that she had all those other kids and didn't need me, I knew the truth was otherwise. It's like the story Jesus tells of the shepherd going off after that one lost sheep. If only I'd tried to meet them halfway and made an attempt to straighten out my life. But the truth is, I didn't want to. I was incapable of it. I didn't know what was wrong with me. I just thought I was crazy.

• • •

At the end of that summer, I went home for a while. But soon enough I was back on the streets. Sometimes my dad would throw me out. Other times I just left. It was more — and less — than just wanderlust or a spirit of adventure that motivated me. I'd be home with my family and just get the overwhelming urge to leave. I felt like I was missing something, but I didn't know what. So I would climb out the window and run to my street corner. Many times I would find no one else there. I'd be alone with nowhere to go, nowhere to sleep. No money. No food. Just homeless.

Sometimes I'd stay with my friend Mike and his mom, Judy. She welcomed me, a broken and confused kid, and I have never forgotten her kindness.

I was the kind of guy that, if you stuck your hand out to feed me, I might bite off your finger. I rebelled against the whole idea of accepting the love and kindness of others. They'd try to help me and I'd steal from them. I'd smash up their house. I'd lie to them and act in ways of which I am, today, deeply ashamed. Judy was probably the only person who went out of her way to help me and care for me and had genuine concern for me, whom I never hurt in any way. I never stole from her or lied to her or damaged her or her belongings.

But I did all that and more to my family and to those closest to me.

My family didn't know I was staying with Judy. After a certain point they would just stop looking for me. I was gone, I was on the run, and even if they looked for me and found me, I'd just run away again. I couldn't stay with anyone for too long a period of time. So I slept anywhere I could. Ideally I'd crash at a friend's house, but if necessary I'd sleep on park benches, on porches, anywhere I could lay my head and maybe keep warm.

One of the lowest points in a childhood with way more valleys than peaks came when I was thirteen and had, as usual, been thrown out of the house by my dad. I had nowhere to go, so my friends Jim and Bill took me in. Their family rented the top floor of a three-decker house on Adams Street. At first they let me stay upstairs, in their room, until their mom figured out that her sons had taken in a tenant and told me I had to leave.

So the boys moved me into the basement. It was kind of cozy. I had a little lounge chair near the boiler that kept me warm, until one of the neighbors discovered me, and I was evicted from the basement.

Jim and Bill were faithful friends, though, and they came up with one last option. They showed me a little trapdoor that opened to a spot under the front porch. It was just an empty space, nothing but dirt, but it was better than sleeping in the street. So thirteen-year-old Jim Wahlberg took up residence under a porch, sleeping on blankets over the cold earth.

I thought I couldn't go any lower than sleeping in the dirt under a porch — but I was wrong.

I remember one time I was thrown out of my family's house in the middle of February. It was the usual scene: "You don't want to be here? You don't want to go along with the rules? Get out!"

No way I was going to sleep on or under porches in sub-zero temperatures. So my sister Michelle snuck me back into the house. I was sleeping soundly on the floor behind the couch when my dad came down. He had to get up at four in the morning to deliver school lunches in his truck. He saw me asleep on the floor. He started screaming.

"Get up. Get out. You ain't welcome here."

And out I went into the frozen predawn, wondering how a father, any father, could kick a son, even one as bad as I was, into the arctic cold. Of course, I didn't see my own part in all this. I just focused on him. How could he do this to me? Poor, poor, pitiful me? Was it tough love, or just an absence of love?

I don't think I ever heard "I love you" pass his lips, unless he had a couple of drinks in him. He worked hard, he drank hard, he screamed loudly, he smoked cigarettes like they were going out of style. (Which, of course, they were.)

He never admitted to being an alcoholic, but he was one. He started drinking as soon as he woke up. Other people would have coffee before breakfast; he would have coffee brandy. When I was a kid, it seemed like my father always had a drink in his hand, usually coffee brandy or beer. He and my mother yelled at each other all the time, though I can't say I recall just what the arguing was about. Frustration, I suppose, and unrealized dreams.

Eventually my mother threw my father out of the house. I wasn't there when it happened. I was either in a foster home or juvenile detention. I confess that sometimes those years blur together, so I'm not sure when exactly this was.

I guess my mom just couldn't take it anymore.

I didn't find out about it till I came home for Christmas and found this guy she'd been seeing making himself at home in our house. Well, in her house. It really wasn't mine anymore.

No one blamed my mom for throwing my dad out. He was not a good husband. Yes, he worked hard and provided. I think that in his mind that constituted the totality of a husband's duty. And as I've mentioned, to his great credit, he stepped up and treated my three oldest siblings as his own.

But I don't ever remember seeing him hug or kiss my mother. I'm sure it happened, but I have no recollection of it. The happy times were few and very far between.

So I come home that Christmas, and what to my wondering eyes should appear but this man who has taken my father's place. Unfortunately for him, my father decides that he's coming home for Christmas, too, and reclaiming his place in the family. The guy gets wind of my father's approach and jumps out the window, which might have hurt, but probably saved him from a thrashing.

My father starts raging at my mother: "This is my house. I bought it. I pay the mortgage. You want to leave? Fine. Leave. I'm staying."

He stayed. She left. Mom and the youngest kids — Tracey, Bob, Donnie, and Mark — moved in with her boyfriend. The older four kids stayed with my dad, though shortly after this my sister Michelle moved in with her boyfriend, too. And I continued on the not-so-merry-go-round of foster homes and institutional housing.

· · ·

By this point, decisions about my life were being made by the Massachusetts Department of Youth Services, not the Wahlberg family. I was shuttled between foster homes and other temporary residences. I lived for a year with a family of Jehovah's Witnesses in Brockton, Massachusetts. They were nice people — they never proselytized me or the other foster kid they'd taken in — but it was the same old thing. Just as water seeks its own level, I gravitated immediately to the kids who smoked pot and drank and hung out to no good end.

I even got a job in Brockton working in a donut shop. It didn't last long. I came into the shop one day, found that no one else was there, stared at the pile of pots and pans and said, "I'm not doing this." I walked out, leaving the doors wide open and the counter unattended.

There were brief intervals in which I was allowed to go home. The Department of Youth Services would call my dad and tell him that I deserved another shot, that I was doing well, that maybe if I reentered a stable domestic routine, I'd snap back to being a normal kid.

But I was never doing well. I was never not drinking. I was never not using drugs. I just wasn't getting caught. If there was an opportunity to steal something, I'd steal it.

This wasn't my father's fault; it was my fault, totally. But the instability of the household sure didn't help. There was zero supervision of us kids. My dad would drink before he went to work — I'm sure he drank whenever he could while at work — and then he'd come home, drink, and pass out. We were on our own — or I should say *they* were, my siblings, since I was seldom around.

My older brother Paul had to be the adult. That became his role in the family. He started working, and he's never stopped. He always wanted to be a chef. As I mentioned earlier, my dad was a good cook when he put his mind to it, but Paul was a star. I'm proud that he grew up to be an executive chef and the culinary brains behind the Wahlburgers chain he owns with Mark and Donnie.

Every time I'd come back for a brief stay with my family, I'd feel more uneasy being around my friends. It ate at me that they were looking down on me. They thought they were better than me. They were drunks and druggies just like I was, but that sense of inferiority that had been building since I was a little kid just grew stronger.

I lacked identity. I remember one of my early runaway experiences when I was hanging out with this criminal-type character named Ricky. He was probably sixteen or seventeen. We were stealing cars. Or, more accurately, he was stealing cars and I was going along for the ride. We watched a guy put a big boombox in his trunk and decided we had to steal that car to get the boombox. We did. After that, Ricky walked around all day long holding the boombox, playing it at an earsplitting volume. It might sound pathetic to you, but that boombox gave him an identity. Girls would talk to him. People on the train would look at him. Now he was somebody.

Ricky came from a family of alcoholics and drug addicts. I stayed with them for a while, sleeping on their back porch, and then I moved on. That's how it was: People would weave in and out of my life, and I'd weave in and out of their lives, and then I'd just find someone else to get drunk and get high with. There was no stability, no permanence.

I couldn't explain the things I did. I thought I was just nuts. Once, my older sister Debbie (who has since passed away) and her boyfriend let me stay with them after I'd been kicked out of the house yet again. And what did I do? I stole from them. They took me in, they gave me food and shelter and love, and I stole from them. I sabotaged myself. By biting the hand that fed me, I was only hurting myself.

But why? I couldn't figure it out. You would think that a person in shame and pain would try to move out of that sorrow and toward something better, but I just burrowed deeper into the pain.

Looking back, I think the main reason is that I lacked a true foundation in the Faith. I had no concept or understanding of a loving God. I didn't realize that God loves us all, even sinners, and that Jesus Christ died for my sins. Just because I make a mistake doesn't mean that God isn't going to love me and forgive me.

I just didn't have a clue.

CHAPTER THREE
DOWN THE HOLE

I was every kind of drunk: manic and morose, sullen and slap-happy, charming and violent. I was just so unpredictable. I could be your best pal or could be chasing you down the street, throwing rocks at you. I could even be stomping you into unconsciousness.

I'm not exaggerating. One of my most shameful episodes happened one night at Ashmont Station. Two kids, probably about my age, were goofing around on the escalator. I yelled at them, "What are you doing? Get outta there." Like it was my train station!

One of them talked back to me. I don't remember what he said, but I was drunk and aggressive. I ran over to him. We had words. The situation went from zero to ninety in about ten seconds. I punched him in the face. He fell down. I started kicking him and then jumping up and down on top of him. I later was told that both his legs were broken.

I was never punished for this, though I knew that the kid's older brother was looking for me. He would have bashed my head into the ground had he caught me. But I was getting pretty good at not getting caught.

I also once hit a guy with a two-by-four for no reason at all. We were both drunk and pathetic. But he got even. He saw me a couple days later — I was blind drunk, surprise, surprise, surprise — and he hit me with a crowbar. Twice.

I woke up in the hospital. I didn't know how I got there, and I didn't know who did it. I'm told that I was unconscious for two days. I escaped from the hospital. It wasn't much of an escape — nothing like the hospital escapes in movies, where guys don scrubs and imitate doctors and push gurneys and slip into empty rooms to avoid detection. I just got up, put on my clothes, and walked out. I went back to Ashmont, walked into the Tara Room, and when I saw this guy sitting at the bar, I knew he was the one who had whacked me.

I went outside and called my friend Spags, the toughest guy in the neighborhood. He was the guy nobody messed with; I'd never seen him lose a fight. He and his brother came right away, stormed into the Tara Room, and beat the crap out of my assailant. From that day forward, every time I saw this poor fella, I extorted money or booze from him.

I still have a scar above my left ear from that attack. I'm sure the other guy has his scars, too.

• • •

The assault that landed me in state prison was actually less violent than either of these cases.

There were three of us: my best friend, Sean, a younger kid, and me. We punched and kicked some random guy and stole his money. Our attitude was that it was the victim's fault. What was he doing at Ashmont Station at two in the morning? (The question of what *we* were doing at Ashmont Station at two in the morning never occurred to us.)

This wasn't my first assault. I'd taken things from people and beaten people up many times before. But this time we had a U.S. Navy sword that we'd stolen. We were fooling around with it as if we were in *Star Wars* or *The Three Musketeers*. We didn't stab the guy, but we did point it at him and tell him to give it up.

It was a terrible thing we did, and stupid, too. By brandishing that sword, a weapon we didn't need and didn't use, we elevated our offense into armed robbery. It cost me five years — five wasted, futile, God-less years. Although our victim landed in the hospital, he recovered, thank God.

I wasn't exactly the canniest fugitive on the lam. It wasn't going to take Sherlock Holmes to track me down. Sean had called me "Jimbo" during the commission of the crime, and I was about the only Jimbo in the neighborhood — or at least the best-known Jimbo as far as local law enforcement personnel were concerned. Like I said, we weren't the smartest criminals who ever lived.

I was hiding at my mom's house on Peverell Street up on Savin Hill. She and her new husband were at work, and my brother Bob snuck me in so I could shower and change my clothes. Bob and Donnie were always doing me favors: loving me, worrying about their big brother out there living on the street. And then I would push them to a point beyond their endurance.

A couple of days after the assault, the cops came by my mom's house looking for me. They knocked on the door. I answered it.

"We're looking for James Wahlberg."

"He's not here."

"Who are you?"

"I'm his brother Bob."

"What's your date of birth?"

I gave them a date that would have made me about ten years old.

Game over.

I was arrested. My previous arrests had been for relatively minor offenses like being drunk and disorderly. This was my first serious offense, or at least the first serious crime I'd been nabbed for. There was no bail and no trial; I pled guilty. And though I was only seventeen, the judge handed down a sentence of three to five years in adult prison.

What? Three to five in prison? Man, I'd been doing this kind of thing my whole life and nobody ever said they'd send me to *prison* for it.

I was the only one who was arrested or punished for the crime. The cops probably suspected Sean, since he was my constant companion, my partner in crime — lots of crimes — but I guess they didn't know he had been with me during that sword-aided armed robbery. I'm no Jimmy Cagney, but I wasn't about to rat on my best friend. I never told on the third guy who was with us, either, and I never will. He was a younger kid whom Sean and I were leading down a very bad path. He looked up to us. What a mistake that was. We were about the worst role models you could find. But I'm glad to say that the third member of our trio is doing okay today.

I wish Sean's story also had a happy ending. It doesn't. He was a nice guy — he really was, despite his criminal record. The trouble came when he drank. Sean was a full-blown alcoholic. He would go through phases. He'd get in trouble for something he'd done while drunk, then he'd just stop drinking, cold turkey. For maybe six months he'd stay in the house and almost never come out. He'd just exercise and watch TV all day. He wanted to prove to himself that he didn't have to drink. And then one day he'd emerge, get drunk, get into a fight, get his head split open and his teeth knocked out, and spiral downward in a cycle of drunkenness and misbehavior until he was ready for the wagon again.

It was just his brokenness. He was my absolute best friend, not just my drinking buddy. We were inseparable. I still ache when I think of Sean.

Years later I ran into Sean when I was working in detox. I was sober and doing well. I was out running an errand for the detox; Sean was driving a cab.

He hailed me. "Hey, buddy, what's up? Come on, hop in."

I got in his cab and we talked. Soon enough the talk turned to drinking.

"Dude, why don't you come to AA?" I said. "Look at me. I found the answer, man. We can do good. We can live a good life."

He scoffed. "Nah, that's boring." As if locking yourself in your room for six months to watch television and prove that you can stop drinking isn't boring?

I never saw him again. He drank himself to death — literally. Sean died in the street from an alcoholic seizure when he was in his thirties.

• • •

I was behind bars before I could legally drink in a bar.

I was sent first to MCI-Walpole, a maximum security state prison. This was ironic: One of my nicknames in the juvenile detention system had been "Jimmy Walpole," and I'm afraid I lived down to it.

I was issued my ID at Walpole and then sent over to MCI-Concord, a medium security state prison that also serves as a classification center. Concord is a beautiful town, made famous by a Revolutionary War battle as well as its distinguished literary residents, such as Henry David Thoreau, Ralph Waldo Emerson, and my distant cousin Nathaniel Hawthorne. MCI-Concord is the oldest state prison for men in Massachusetts, and it boasts some impressive architectural features, but I'm afraid a teenage inmate doesn't really notice or care about these things.

MCI-Concord is where the authorities determine where you'll serve your sentence. They interview and evaluate you and then either ship you out or keep you in Concord. Guys try to toe the line during classification because if you don't, you'll be sent to a higher security prison. I'd been sentenced to Walpole, but that prison is for the most hardened and incorrigible prisoners, many of them doing life. There aren't many guys doing three to five in Walpole. The assumption was that I'd do time in a somewhat less crazy place.

After a couple of months they sent me to MCI-Norfolk, another medium security prison, where I promptly got into trouble and was shipped over to Walpole, where I would serve the rest of my sentence. And I served every last day of that sentence. I did most of it in "the hole."

I hadn't been in Walpole long before I got into trouble. A

friend of mine (like so many of my friends from this era, he has since died of an overdose) stole a pair of sneakers from another guy. This was a common kind of theft. Prisoners would order sneakers or other goods through the commissary, a guy working in the commissary would steal them, and the prison would have to buy the first guy another pair of sneakers. It's like a 2-for-1 deal. Well, my friend stole this particular pair of sneakers from a guy who'd already stolen them from someone else. They fought, and my buddy stabbed him. The alarms sounded. My friend threw the knife into the shower and kept walking.

The guards knew he had done it, but they hadn't seen him dispose of the knife. So I slipped into the shower, picked up the knife — it was a prison-made shiv, really a glorified piece of metal — and threw it down the drain. That made me an accessory to that crime.

I couldn't keep my big mouth shut. Our cells consisted of a bed, a sink, a toilet, maybe a TV or a shelf for books or whatever. There was a vent behind the toilet. The guards used to go behind the cell block and listen to our conversations through the vents. That was a basic investigative tool. While they were eavesdropping, they heard me hiss to another guy: "Tell him don't worry. I got rid of the knife. They'll never find it." An hour later the guards came to my cell and hauled me off to the hole.

The hole, aka the segregation unit, is a prison within a prison. It's a punitive place for guys who commit serious infractions — killing, stabbing, maiming, rioting, fighting, attacking guards, getting caught with drugs — while they're in prison. The hole is a separate unit way at the end of the facility. You have a single cell, smaller than a regular cell, with cement walls. There are two doors: a little bar door and then a solid door. The only aperture is a small window that permits you to see directly in front of your cell but provides no peripheral vision. You're locked in for twenty-three hours a day, seven days a week.

Once a day, for an hour, you are led from your cell, handcuffs behind your back, to what looks like a dog kennel, consisting of a row of about twenty adjacent cages with fencing on the sides and on top. They're perhaps six feet wide, twelve feet high, and thirty feet long. It's one man to a cage. Once inside the cage your handcuffs are removed and you are free to walk back and forth, pacing like … well, like an animal in a cage. That's how you're treated, and that's how you come to behave.

It was strange, living there day after day, talking to or shouting at or being shouted at by people you never saw. Every once in a while you'd be taken out of your cell, but if I'm in cell five and you're in cell four, I wouldn't pass your cell on my way out, so I could live next to you for a year, two years, five years, and never even see your face.

The inmates communicated with one another by screaming as loud as they could, the sound carrying through the small window. The communication was not, as you might guess, of a very high level. Mostly it consisted of prisoners trying to incite other prisoners to do things that would get them in even more trouble.

Let's go on a hunger strike! Let's throw feces at the guards!

Still, with nothing but time on their hands, the prisoners had devised some other, more ingenious methods of communication. The segregation unit had four tiers, two upstairs and two downstairs. These guys found ways to send notes or drugs downstairs through holes dug into the pipes that ran along the walls.

Even criminals, even the lowest of the low, crave human contact. Here I was, an eighteen-year-old kid, and I was alone in a cell. I couldn't even see the guy in the cell next to me. All I could do was eat, sleep, read books, and start trouble.

As for the books, they weren't exactly the classics. They were all about crime, and I don't mean Dostoyevsky's *Crime and Punishment*. You could read multiple books a day, sometimes over and over if they were good. Then you'd fling the book out the little window of your cell to the next guy.

Being in the hole was a form of torture, no doubt about it. It was sensory deprivation. It was inhumane. But even though I've been through it, I still wonder: What do you do with an inmate who stabs a guard or a fellow inmate? You can't just leave him in his cell. You can't let him roam freely through the population. He has to be isolated. Yet while I have no problem with extra punishment for such a man, you can't treat people like animals and expect them to act like human beings.

Some of the guards took joy in making things worse for us. I realize they were spending their days with vile and violent men, but sometimes they didn't seem much better. There was this one inmate who'd been exiled to the hole because he had assaulted a nurse. He was mentally ill. As a protest, he lit his cell on fire. The guard stuck his key in the keyhole and broke it off. The guy died in his cell fire.

We had two sadistic guards who worked the overnight shift. These creeps would listen at the back of our cells and say things to us to drive us crazy. They'd make weird noises to get us to think we were hearing things, or they'd cuss at us that we were "worthless pieces of shit." On a whim they'd close the doors at a time when they were supposed to be open.

After a while you might form relationships — I don't know if you could call them friendships — with some of the other guys in the hole with you, but the baseness and brutality was never far from the surface. A lot of these guys were evil or nuts. Let's say an informant or child molester — the two lowest forms of life in prison — was put in the hole. The other inmates would chant for hours, urging him to kill himself. "Hang it up, Charlie, hang it up. Hang it up, Charlie, hang it up." Imagine listening to that — imagine chanting that — all day long.

If you're new on the unit, the "veterans" are going to make you sing that song. And you'll sing it. Because if you don't, you'll be the next target of their harassment.

There were some real characters in the hole, though by that word I don't mean to suggest that they were winsome or charming or amusing. There was Dave, a guy who was doing time with his brother. He fancied himself a singer, and he wasn't half bad. He'd sing oldies like "Under the Boardwalk" as loud as he could, putting on a concert for us with all the passion and conviction of Frank Sinatra. That was our entertainment for the day.

Less entertainingly, I was in the hole next to a guy I'd first met in juvenile detention. This guy worshiped the devil. I'm not saying that metaphorically; he really did. He had killed an old woman in a particularly gruesome fashion. And there he was, in the cell next to mine. It made me glad the hole consisted of solitary cells, because he was so deranged he might have murdered his cellmate just for fun.

If it's true that you can't choose your relatives, it's just as true that you can't choose the guys in the prison cell next door. So I played chess with my deranged next-door neighbor. Not face-to-face, of course. We made our own chessboard and pieces and pushed it back and forth on the floor outside our cells. You'd make your move and send it on back. He wasn't a bad chess player, but I dearly hope he is never released from prison. He's just too scary.

Your common bond with the other prisoners is that you've all convinced yourselves that you're victims of circumstance. It's someone else's fault that you're in Walpole or you're in the hole. It's never your own fault.

Then the troubles just mount. You're in a downward spiral and it seems like there's no way out. I was always trying to impress someone, even in prison, and to get them to think a certain way about me. I wanted them to think: "He's a solid guy. He's a stand-up guy. He don't take no crap from nobody."

The way you do that is to put on a tough and hardened front. And if you have to fight, you fight.

I remember a fight I had at Walpole with a guy named Leo. I was in my cell in population and he was sweeping and mopping the tiers. I threw something on the floor. Now, my attitude was: "What do you care if I throw something on the tier? That's not directed toward you. That's directed toward them. Do you work for them?"

Leo was supposedly a connected guy who knew big people. He'd been in and out of prison his whole life. And he saw this as an opportunity. I was a kid. Maybe I weighed 130 pounds sopping wet. No way could I beat him up. So he thought he'd punk me and make himself look good.

I came out of my cell to make a phone call. Right in front of a guard Leo took a swing at me, which is not a move that's really accepted in prison. You want to fight somebody? Don't do it in front of a guard; do it when nobody is around. We fought, and they hauled me back to the hole. Leo didn't get in trouble.

I also did plenty of things that tarnished my reputation with the other inmates. Once I got into an argument with a guard, a big guy. We had words, and there was no way I could let him talk to me like that. I told him to "eff" off. He said, "Come on,

I'll take off my badge. Let's go in this closet and settle it." I went in there, and I didn't do anything. I didn't take a swing at him. He got the upper hand on me and made me look bad. My reputation took a hit. The attitude among the other inmates was, "You let him do that to you? You're a punk."

Guys in prison are constantly looking for weakness. For a chink in the armor. They elevate their own status by demeaning yours. It's a nightmare that you can't wake up from.

In response to inmate lawsuits, the prison adopted a phase system for segregation. If you behaved, you'd be sent to a lower level of segregation. For instance, you start in 10 Block. If you behave, you move to 9 Block, which has two-man cells, and as you progress, the ultimate end is that you are transferred from maximum security Walpole into the population in a medium security prison.

I made it out of the hole briefly. I graduated from 10 Block to 9 Block — which the authorities renamed Phase 1 and Phase 2, for no apparent reason other than to confuse all involved. Phase 3 was a transfer to Norfolk, where within a period of weeks I would have been released into the general population. But I screwed up and was returned to 10 Block.

The problem is that once you're in the hole, boredom and the desire to impress your neighbors lead you to do stupid things. You might throw something at a guard, for instance. This triggers a search of your cell. If you meekly submit, the other guys are going to give you a hard time. They'll make your life even more miserable than it already is. So when the extraction team comes to remove you in order for them to shake down your cell, you holler, "I'm not coming out! Come and get me!"

Your wish is their command. They tear-gas you, and the

guys in Darth Vader uniforms with shields and billy clubs come in and beat you. Nobody can see you. The other inmates have no way of witnessing your stupid act of masochism. I could be down on my knees with my hands behind my back the whole time. It could all be an act.

In a way, it was all an act. I was trying to act tough, to create the illusion that I was a badass. And I did that because their opinion of me — the opinion of these murderers and rapists and degenerates — meant more to me than my opinion of myself. I didn't even have an opinion of myself. I was not a free-thinker; I wasn't any kind of thinker at all. I would just steal your idea, which is why I wanted you to think I was a bad dude who took no crap from guards or anyone else.

You couldn't let a guard disrespect you. That was a cardinal rule. If you didn't mouth off to them immediately, you'd be tagged: "You let that guy talk to you like that? What are you, a punk?" The mental pressure was just so intense. You did not want to fall out of favor with the other prisoners — hardened criminals that could kill you or torture you or make your life a living hell, just for one mistake.

And remember: All this is happening to a kid who never really developed intellectually. My mental capacity was stunted. I'd filled my brain with drugs and alcohol and been bashed in the head with bricks and crowbars, and I'd crashed stolen cars and damaged myself in ways that are hard to comprehend. Because I was broken.

It's almost like I didn't have a personality, or my personality was that of a chameleon. In the chow hall at Walpole State Prison, the tables were assigned by the inmates, not the guards. There was the Southie table, the Charlestown table, the gangster table, the black guys table, the East Boston Italian table. If you weren't one of them, you couldn't sit there.

I'm eighteen years old, on one of my occasional breaks from the hole, and I'm walking past all these tables on the way to the Dorchester table. I knew a lot of these guys from the streets or from juvenile detention, and I'm a talkative guy, so I'd stop at the tables to say hi to guys I knew. And my personality would adapt with each conversation. My tone and language would change at each table. With the Italian guys I'd be gesturing like Uncle Vinny, talking with my hands; with the black guys I'd be talking like a brother.

When I got older I looked back and realized that this adaptability was really about my need for acceptance, for love, for people's good opinion — even if the good opinion was that of a gangster. It's like I wasn't quite a person. I didn't have my own identity.

My mother came to visit me — once. She didn't recognize me as her child. I was like an animal. Feral. As she tells the story, she pulled over on the highway on her way home, crying tears of overwhelming sadness. She pledged to herself that day that she would never visit her son in a place like that again. And she didn't.

• • •

I've remained lifelong friends with some of the guys I met in prison. And I developed lifelong animosities, too, though as a man of God, I labor to dissolve those.

Resentments are a funny thing. You can't really control them. Someone mentions a name and your immediate response, based on your experience with that person, is negative. But that's not how we're meant to live. Today, I look at that person I once "hated" and realize that he was broken, just as I was. I look at his circumstances, the influences in his life. I try to understand. When you're young and dumb, that's so hard to do. It comes with faith, with having a relationship with God, who helps you put yourself in somebody else's shoes.

I'm a sinner. I'm far from perfect. If you mention certain names to me, my first thought is still negative. But the most difficult of all the lessons Jesus Christ taught was, "Love thine enemies." Man is that ever difficult. God does not make it easy. But each of us is blessed with the capacity for love and mercy and forgiveness.

It took me a long time to learn this. I wasn't brought up that way. I was raised to be judgmental, not forgiving. I wasn't raised to love my enemies. Who is, really? But with Christ, all things are possible.

CHAPTER FOUR
THE FACE OF GOD

I was to be released from Walpole on a Monday. The Friday before, they let me out of the hole for the first time in years. I was moved into the new-man block, because if I went crazy and killed a bunch of people upon my release, the authorities didn't want to have to explain why I'd gone directly from twenty-three-hour-a-day maximum security lockup to the streets.

I'm in the new-man unit the weekend before I'm let out. Everyone is walking around freely. A guard comes over to me. He says, "Hey, that guy in Cell 7 raped kids. Feel free to make a move."

The message was clear: Do what you want. The guard would look the other way. Okay, if you say so. I slipped out of my cell, entered Cell 7, found no one there, and set fire to a box of papers the child-rapist had on his bed. Then I slipped back into my cell. The guy wasn't in there at the time. I just burned his belongings. Once again, I was looking for acceptance and approval, even from a guard I didn't know and who was, in the prison world, an enemy.

Two days later I was out on the streets, ready to see my mother for the first time in years. It's a miracle I didn't get out and just start killing people. I was so full of rage and not mentally stable by any stretch of the imagination.

Arthur, my oldest brother, picked me up from Walpole State Prison just two days following my Saturday act of arson. Our first stop was the Tara Room on Ashmont. I was back on my block, and finally old enough to drink legally in a bar. Arthur and I ordered a couple of beers. Pat, the owner of the Tara Room, a tapster straight from the Old Sod, came over. He put the beer down in front of me and said, "Enjoy it, because it's the only one you'll ever have in my bar." I'd been in the Tara Room for five minutes and had already worn out my welcome. I knew what it was about, though. One of the last things I did before I went to prison was walk around all day with a golf club in my hand. That night, Pat found the head of that golf club on the front seat of his car. I'd smashed out the windows while in a blackout.

Arthur and I drained our beers and headed over to visit my mother.

As I mentioned earlier, my mother had moved to the first floor of a three-decker on Peverell Street. She lived with a man named Mark, whom she would marry. My sister Tracey and my brothers Bob, Donnie, and Mark lived with them.

Mom says that within a minute of seeing me, she knew I'd be going back to prison. All she could think of while I was sitting at her kitchen table was that she couldn't wait for me to leave.

I was out for almost exactly six months from the day of my release. For those six months I was either in a blackout or a grayout the entire time. In a blackout, I was awake, alert, eyes open, but I wasn't fully aware of what was going on around me. I would get an idea in my head that usually had me showing up at the place in the world where I was least wanted. Say, for example, at my girlfriend's apartment at three in the morning, or a bar from which I'd been banned for life. My head would lean forward and my body would follow, and I might not even understand where I was going. But it was always a mistake.

A grayout was similar, though I'd be functioning at a somewhat higher level. To observers, I didn't seem to be quite so wasted. An alcoholic is saturated in alcohol, so he never knows what effect the next drink is going to have on him. I could go into a bar, have two beers, and blackout, and the next thing you know I'm throwing a bottle at the bartender and punching the guy next to me, and I'm not even aware of what I'm doing. Or I might have twenty-five drinks and just pass out harmlessly. You never know because you're always under the influence. But when you come to, there's a rush of fear and paranoia that hits you all at once, and the only thing that's going to make that anxiety and fear go away is the comfort that a drink brings you. You down it, and that warm feeling goes up the back of your spine. It's not enjoyment. It's not exhilaration. It's medication.

For six months I consumed as much alcohol as was humanly possible. I consumed as many drugs as was humanly possible. I did anything that I could get my hands on. My favorite was cocaine, because it kept me awake, and as long as I was awake I could keep drinking.

Before my incarceration I'd been living with a girl in the

projects in South Boston. She actually visited me in prison. And when I got out I didn't even want to see her at first. All I wanted was booze and drugs.

Toward the tail end of these six months, I got in touch with my former girlfriend. She was still living in the Old Harbor projects, this time with a woman whose husband was in prison. She took me in. Old Harbor housed poor whites, though today it's full of poor people of all colors. If you've seen the film *The Departed*, you've seen these projects.

At that time, Old Harbor was a nest of drug addicts. People came in and out of my life, the common denominator being our craving for, and consumption of, drugs. I don't know that you'd call these people friends. They were running partners. We were all on this sinking ship and I suppose some bonds of loyalty might develop, but it was all based in fear.

That's how I met Billy. He shot ten bags of heroin in his arm every morning just to get regular. Billy wasn't getting high; he just didn't want to be sick.

The one and only time I ever shot drugs was with this guy. Using whatever intellectual capacity I had in my brain at that time, I calculated I was better off doing what he was doing than what I was doing. Because when I woke in the morning, I was afraid of everything. I needed a drink to quell the fear. Billy, on the other hand, woke up possessed. Nothing could stand in his way of shooting those ten bags. In the morning we'd go shoplifting. He would walk into a department store and just take anything he wanted. He knew exactly where to go to sell it to get his heroin. Then he would get me my first couple of drinks so I could do the things that he was doing. Our lives were spent, day after day, trying to figure out how we were going to get high.

I was as broken a young man as you could ever meet.

So I made the conscious decision that I was going to start shooting heroin. Billy, to his credit, actually tried to talk me out of it. I shot cocaine instead — something I would never recommend to anybody. It was the craziest thing in the world to do. But I did it. And then I got drunk like I did every other day.

That night I got arrested for robbing a Boston cop's house in the middle of the night. It's not like I was going to mastermind a bank robbery; I was in no condition for anything requiring more than a minimal amount of brain cells. I was just wandering around, checking people's doors. I found one open and walked right in. It was a little apartment in South Boston. No one was home. I collected whatever resalable belongings I could find — a VCR, stuff like that. I really don't recall the particulars.

As I'm walking out the door, it occurs to me that there might be something drinkable in the fridge. Sure enough, there is. So I pop open a beer and sit down at the kitchen table to enjoy it. I'm passed out at the kitchen table when the apartment's resident comes home. Just my luck, it's a cop and his partner on their coffee break. They proceed to beat the living crap out of me.

I was charged with a home invasion, which carries a life sentence. That is a very serious crime, and although in this instance it was more a case of a blacked-out drunk staggering into the first unlocked house he could find, I was facing the harshest penalty there is short of capital punishment.

I had a public defender, as always; I never once retained a private attorney. I pled guilty. They had me dead to rights. No member of my family was in that courtroom. They'd pretty much given up on me, and I can't blame them. My future looked awfully bleak.

The cop whose place I'd busted into — and who had busted me up pretty bad — actually spoke up for me. He said: "Look at this kid. He's a mess. Get him some help." He wasn't opposed to me going to prison, and he certainly wasn't sorry for whipping my butt, but he thought a potential life sentence was ridiculous. He was an old-school guy, a neighborhood guy. He was satisfied with the beating he'd given me. "You did that. I did this. Good enough for me."

We plea-bargained it down to breaking and entering, a nonviolent crime which carried a sentence of six to nine years. That's pretty stiff, but, then, I had a past.

With good behavior I might get out in three to four years, but when had I ever behaved? Even though I had dropped out of school early, I could do the math. Nine years in prison meant that I'd be over thirty when I got out. That sounded ancient. I needed a plan.

I went to Walpole for a couple of days and then was shipped to MCI-Concord for classification. That's where I would meet Father Jim Fratus. It's where I would start creating the illusion that I was on the right track, and then the illusion would become reality. And it's where, by the grace of God, and the intercession of one or two of his saints, I, too, would become a man of God.

• • •

First thing I realized was that if I had to serve this sentence in Walpole, I'd be back in the hole and do all nine years. Because there's really no way out of that cycle. I was paranoid. I was crazy, really. And the anxiety meter is always 100 at Walpole. At any moment somebody could pull out a knife and stab somebody or attack a guard. A riot could break out. You could get tear-gassed. You always had to be on your toes, even about stepping on someone else's toes, because guys were quick to take offense and demand redress. Everyone was living the way I was living, worried about their image and what fellow criminals thought of them.

Some things carried over from my first prison sentence to my second. Leo, the guy who got upset when I threw something on the floor at Walpole for him to sweep up, was at Concord on my second go-round. Oh boy, I thought, more trouble. But someone, I still don't know who, approached Chucky, a legit gangster who carried a lot of weight within Concord. People listened to him, respected him. This unknown intermediary told Chucky that Leo and I had a history, that we hated each other, and suggested that maybe Chucky could broker a peace.

He did. He arranged a sit-down with the two of us to smooth things over. Now, a sit-down with Chucky wasn't really a sit-down. He was in constant motion and was famous for walking all day at a high rate of speed. So Leo and I accompanied Chucky on one of his walks.

He said: "Look, you're a good guy, he's a good guy. (I didn't think Leo was a good guy, but I held my tongue.) Mistakes were made. Say your piece and then shake hands and move on."

We did what Chucky asked. And though we didn't become friends, we weren't enemies any longer. If we walked past each other we would say hi, which is a very important matter of etiquette in prison, for to fail to say hi is disrespectful and invites trouble.

Chucky couldn't help me with Crazy Bobby, though. That was a problem I had to handle myself.

One of the bad things about MCI-Concord is that since pretty much everyone who is sentenced to prison goes through there at least for a brief time, you'll probably run into your enemies from the streets. Bobby was a tough, mean, burly, severe drug addict and alcoholic I'd met on the streets. He hung with an insane, cocaine-crazed maniac who used to drive around in his car for days on end, high on coke. What a pair they made.

Anyway, my friend Paul and I once were in possession of some stolen jewelry. We didn't steal it from the jewelry store; we stole it from the jewelry-store thief. He was a younger kid who used to go into the stores, ask to see the gold bracelets, and then grab them and run as fast as he could. Paul and I took one of his gold-bracelet hauls simply because we could. He was lower on the pecking order, and in that amoral world, the big fish eat the small fish.

Unfortunately, we were small fish to Crazy Bobby and the cocaine driver.

Those two set us up to sell the gold to another guy. We four drove to the guy's house together, and only Crazy Bobby went in. He came out a few minutes later with this story about how the guy had robbed him. He didn't even bother making this lie look believable. I could see a bracelet sticking out of his pocket.

We called him on it. And he proceeded to thrash me and Paul. He smacked us around like rag dolls. He was one bad dude. Needless to say, we never got the stolen bracelets back.

Well, who do I see one day at Concord but Crazy Bobby. I went to a friend of mine.

"Dude, I need a knife."

"Whattaya need a knife for? I'm not givin' you a knife unless you tell me what's goin' on."

"I need it for that dude over there."

"Bobby? A knife's not gonna help you. He'll kill you. I grew up with that kid. He's the toughest dude I ever met in my life.

Just figure out a way to be friends."

I don't know if Bobby was really the kind of guy who was capable of having friends, but at least I didn't want him to be an enemy. So I acted like nothing had ever happened. Which was weird at first: to act like that whipping never happened. He'd say something fresh now and then, but I'd ignore it. What choice did I have? I just had to grin and take it. It was clear that he was running the show, and there was nothing I could do. He'd tear me limb from limb if we fought. Eventually he got transferred, and I remained in possession of all my limbs.

The friends I made in prison who are still friends were trying to do easy time. They weren't trying to be tough guys. They were dangerous — some were bank robbers, some were stone-cold killers — but if you were their friend, they were the nicest guys in the world. Crime was just a job to them. That is deeply immoral and deranged, no doubt about it, but it does illustrate the complexity of human beings. There is a divine spark in even the worst of sinners.

• • •

Every big moment in my life was pushing me toward God.

Left to my own devices, I ran into nothing but trouble. But when I let God take over, my life changed.

And one of his priests and one of his saints pointed the way for me.

Here I was in prison again. I'm twenty-two years old, no education, no hopes, staring at a six- to nine-year prison sentence. If I messed up here and had to serve the whole sentence, I'd be thirty-one when I got out. I'd be a relic with one foot in the grave. So what was I going to do?

The Big Hustle, of course. I had to create the illusion that I was trying to change. If I didn't, I'd have squandered my entire youth. I had to shorten this sentence. I needed to give the appearance of being a good boy, a model prisoner, a young man bent on self-improvement.

This was all BS. I just wanted to get out of prison and resume my criminal ways. But to create the illusion, I started going to Alcoholics Anonymous meetings. I went to therapy groups and said what I thought they wanted to hear.

That's when Father Jim Fratus, one of the greatest men I have ever known, approached me. He didn't give me any hard sell. He just told me that he had an opening in the chapel for a janitor, a handyman, a cleanup guy to sweep the floors and empty the trash. Would I be interested?

Well, why not? This looked like the perfect hustle. The guy was a priest. I figured he's probably as naive as a newborn baby. I can con him out of anything: cigarettes, food, access to the phone. Plus I'll get to hide away from this crazy place in a quiet chapel. It'd give me a chance to think, to be by myself. So, sure, Father, I'll do it.

I took the job. Then little by little, Father Fratus drew me in. He said: "Hey, I need you to clean up after Mass Saturday night. Since you have to be there anyway, you may as well come to Mass." Slowly, week by week, he tried to bring me home to the Faith: a faith that was mine by inheritance but about which I knew less than zero.

One day he told me that we were having a special visitor at MCI-Concord: Mother Teresa.

"Oh, that's great, Father," I said. "That's awesome." Pause. "Who's Mother Teresa?"

I really had no idea who she was. Now, not only was I Catholic, at least nominally, but you'd have to be living under a rock in the 1980s not to know who Mother Teresa was: the tiny Albanian nun, founder of the Missionaries of Charity, who had devoted her life to caring for and loving the poor in Calcutta, India. She had won the Nobel Peace Prize and was probably the second most well-known Catholic in the world, behind only the pope. A few years after her death she was canonized and is now known as Saint Teresa of Calcutta.

But to Jim Wahlberg, inmate #44563 of MCI-Concord, she was "Who?"

Turns out she would come in part due to an invitation from Donald Ouimet, a prisoner who had once been a Franciscan monk and who had written to ask if she'd visit. "If it is God's will," she wrote to him, "I will be able to come to you."

It was God's will.

The day came for Mother Teresa's visit: June 4, 1988. I saw her from a distance, walking through the quad inside this medium security state prison with its imposing 40-foot walls that seemed to say, You Will Never Leave.

Here's this little seventy-seven-year-old lady walking toward me, surrounded by all these important people: the governor of Massachusetts, the warden, the commissioner of the Department of Corrections. Mother Teresa was five feet tall if she stood on the tips of her toes, her moth-eaten sweater had holes in it, and her sandals looked like she'd been wearing them since the time of Christ. As she got closer I could see her pockets were stuffed with money, as if people were trying to buy their way into heaven.

It comes time for Mass, which is held in the MCI-Concord gymnasium. Thanks to Father Fratus, I'm walking in the procession — e, Jim Wahlberg, the armed robber, the breaker and enterer.

Cardinal Bernard Law, archbishop of Boston, is presiding. He's wearing his miter hat and sitting on the dais in his cathedra, the bishop's chair. There is a fancy chair up there for Mother Teresa, too, and the cardinal beckons for her to sit with him.

But she shakes her head no, modestly refusing the offer.

Instead, she stays with us. The inmates. The scariest people I have ever met in my life. We are on our knees, and she and the sisters from her order are on their knees. Brothers and sisters before Christ. These guys are prisoners and rapists and murderers and bank robbers and drug dealers and just general scumbags like me. The scourge of the earth, most people would consider us. And Mother Teresa stays with us and prays with us.

For the first time in my life, I saw the face of Christ. The face of love. Mother Teresa knew that we weren't just inmates. Prisoners. The wretched of the earth. We had names, we had stories, we had souls. When asked by the press why she had come, she responded simply, "You must find the face of God on the faces of these prisoners."

• • •

What were the names of those prisoners to whom the faces belonged?

One was Mike, a guy from Charlestown. Mike was a bank robber from a long line of bank robbers. His brother, Steve, was locally famous, or maybe I should say infamous. In 1979, in a truly appalling crime, Steve stood on a rooftop in the projects near the historic spot of Bunker Hill and shot Darryl Williams, a black football player for Jamaica Plain High, for no other reason than that he was black. Darryl Williams was paralyzed for life.

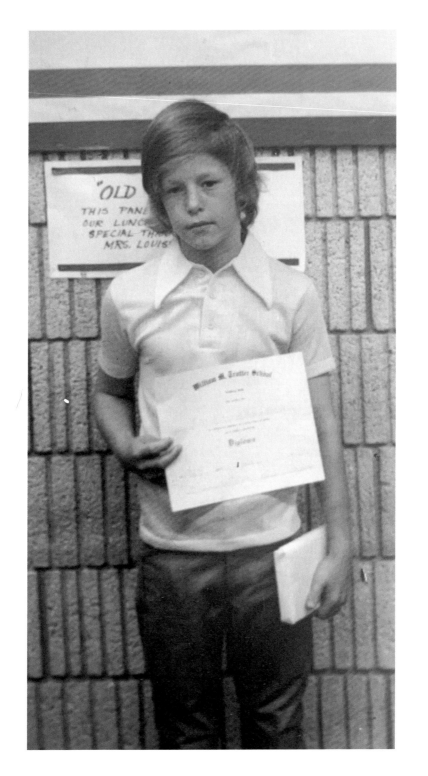

Family photo c. 1974. Back row: Debbie, Michelle, Arthur. Middle Row: Paul, Jim, Tracey. Bottom Row: Bob, Mark, Donnie.

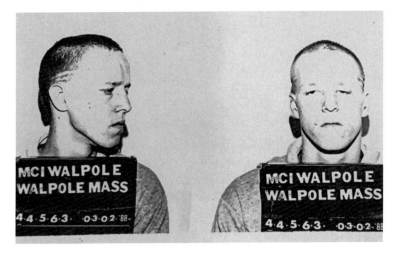

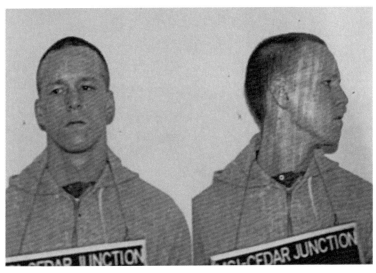

News photo of Mother Teresa's visit to MCI-Concord. This visit had a powerful impact on Jim, who was an inmate at the time. PHOTO BY PAUL C. CLERICI

Jim at his confirmation, which took place at MCI-Plymouth Forestry Camp, 1989.

Jim with his wife, Benerada ("Benny" to her friends), at a friend's wedding in 2010.

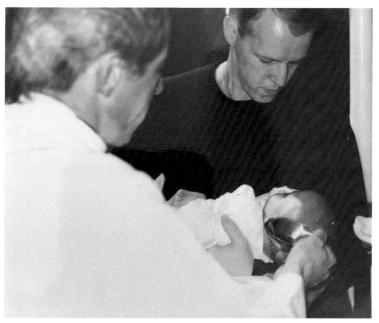

Father Jim Fratus baptizes Jim Wahlberg's son Daniel (April 1993).

Jim with Benerada and their three children (from left to right) Daniel, Kyra, and Jeffrey.

Jim with (from right to left) Jim Caviezel, Kevin King, Mike Sweeney, and Raymond Schidtke in Las Vegas, May 2, 2015.

Mark and Jim Wahlberg prepare for the World Meeting of Families with Pope Francis in Philadelphia, September 2015.

Jim directing the film *What about the Kids?* (August 2019).

Jim with parents who lost their children to overdose, DEA headquarters in Arlington, Virginia (May 2, 2017).

That's Charlestown. It's full of criminals. It is — or certainly was then — very Irish Catholic, a lot like South Boston. But Charlestown was famous for its code of silence. You could kill a guy in front of ten people on a street corner and not one of the witnesses would give up your name. I'm not a huge fan of the Ben Affleck movie *The Town*, but it does capture a bit of what Charlestown was like. Just generation after generation of Irish Catholics who made their living, so to speak, robbing banks and shooting people. It was crazy.

Well, Mike, my buddy at MCI-Concord, was a legit Catholic. A believer. He'd grown up in the insanity of multigenerational crime and dysfunction. He did the crime and he did the time, but can we really blame him entirely for following the well-trod path that led to prison?

There was Paul, an Italian guy from East Boston who was doing time with his brother Joe, a bank robber and a great guy. I know, that may strike you as odd, but believe me: Some of these guys, if they were your friend, were the most loyal and decent people you could know. If they were not your friend … well, that was a different story.

Joe was a close talker. We're sitting in the MCI-Concord dining room and he's got his face right up to mine. We're not trading secrets or anything, but he's a private guy who likes private conversations. Another guy sits at our table and starts telling a mocking story about someone else. Joe thinks he's talking about me, so he grabs a fork and clutches the kid by the shirt and says, "What did you say?"

"No, no, Joe," I say. "He's not talking about me; he's talking about someone else." Joe mumbles an apology and lets the guy go. But that's how he was: loyal to a fault. He's still a friend.

Brendan McNeill was there, too. He's dead now. But Brendan

was with me the first time it ever occurred to me *not* to get high.

Brendan was from Charlestown. He was a big, lovable, goofy guy — a teddy bear — but also dangerous. He was Charlestown to the core, and in Charlestown you weren't anybody till you'd robbed a bank. Brendan was also a drug addict. We were cellmates at MCI-Concord, biding our time and waiting for another guy from Charlestown to make a drug delivery. But this was no ordinary handing over of an illicit substance. This was a prison drug transfer — the passing of a package. Which means this other guy had swallowed the package and we were waiting for him to excrete it.

I don't remember what it was: probably weed or pills. But there we were on St. Patrick's Day, 1988, two addicts waiting for another addict to take a dump so we could smoke or swallow or snort an illegal and dangerous substance. You can't get much lower than that.

The guy couldn't push it out. Brendan and I waited. Meanwhile I had an epiphany. What am I doing? Have I sunk this low? I said to Brendan, "This is crazy, man. We should stop getting high."

The guy eventually got it out. Brendan did the drugs. I didn't.

God was there that day. I haven't been high since. I started going to AA meetings later that month, and while it was in part for show, I refrained from drugs and alcohol. I'm sorry to say that Brendan was later killed in a drug deal that went bad. (As if all drug deals aren't bad to start with.) The guy who delivered the package the hard way is also dead.

• • •

That moment with Mother Teresa changed my life.

I just looked at her and for the first time in my life I saw true humility. I saw love. I saw saintliness.

After Mass she told the inmates: "Remember that God loves you tenderly. You can make this place another Nazareth because Jesus is here, too. If there is any bitterness, get rid of it. Get it out. I will pray for you. I will not forget you. I love you. God bless you."

I didn't understand everything that had happened, but I knew I wanted to know more about it. Right after that I went to Father Jim Fratus and said I wanted to learn more about my faith. And I can only imagine that he went back to his office and said, "Check that box — I got one."

We started confirmation classes. Then the powers-that-be in the prison system decided to transfer me to the medium security facility in Gardner, Massachusetts, with its forty-foot fences, five deep, with razor wire. Despite the word "medium," there was really nothing moderate about it. The priest at Gardner tutored me, but before I could make my confirmation I was transferred again, this time to the minimum security prison known as the Plymouth Forestry Camp, deep in the woods.

All the while I was changing. I wasn't hustling anyone. I didn't care about putting on a false front. I was far from a saint — all the time I had to fight the temptation to cut corners, to think about worldly things, to dream about getting stuff.

But the deeper change in me was as plain as the nose on my face. When people looked at me, they didn't see my scowling Boston mug. They saw a glow. They saw peace. They saw love.

I completed the process and was ready to be confirmed at MCI-Plymouth Forestry Camp. It was the summer of 1989. I called my mother and said: "Mom, I'm going to make my confirmation here in prison. I'd really love it if you could come."

She was hesitant. When she'd seen me at MCI-Walpole, she'd made a promise to herself that she'd never see me in prison again. I told her I'd changed. And that Plymouth Forestry Camp was different than Walpole. It was less scary, less violent, more human.

She thought about it for a while. Then she said yes. And to this day — even as her memory is fading — she talks almost rapturously about what she saw at my confirmation.

I realize that she has only so many stories about me which are good. But whenever I visit her now, she recalls that day, that moment. After the Mass at which I was confirmed, they had a little party for me, with barbecue and a cake. It was really nice.

Today my mother says: "I just watched you walk around that room. I watched the way you talked to people. The way you smiled. I knew that was my son. That was my son. That other guy I visited in prison — that wasn't him. I don't know who he was. The guy who came to my house after he got out the first time — I didn't know who he was, either. But this guy at the confirmation and the party — I recognized him. That was my son. I knew then that you were going to be okay."

I'm not ashamed to say that my eyes well up with tears every time she tells that story. Her maternal instincts toward me returned after that day. It was God's doing. God was showing us what is possible with him in our lives.

Shortly after that I was up for parole. Mom wrote a letter to the parole board. Now, you have to understand something. Alma Wahlberg had spoken to and corresponded with officials in the criminal justice system before. And her message was always, "Lock him up!"

It really was. On more than one occasion with more than one of her sons, she had gone to court and said, in effect: "Help me. I can't control him. I don't know what to do. This isn't working. Put him in jail."

She knew that we'd be safer behind bars. We were out of control and were either going to hurt or kill ourselves, or hurt or kill somebody else. Or we were going to do something so bad that we'd be put away in prison for a very long time.

But this time Mom's message was different. She wrote the parole board and said: "Look, I'm not the mother who lies for her kids. I'm not that mother who thinks her kids can do no wrong. I'm not the mother who's going to tell you a story that just isn't true. But before you stands a man of God. This is not the same person who went into your prison. He is healed. He has found God. He has gotten sober. He is committed to living a good life."

The parole board couldn't have cared less. It's all blah blah blah to them. But this meant the world to me. It was validation from the hardest person in the world to convince that I had changed.

Ultimately, the parole board did release me. But their message was a bit different from my mother's. They said, in effect,:"Here's the deal. We know who you are. We have a thick folder on you. You haven't gotten into any trouble since you've been here this time. So we're going to let you go. But we'll see you when you get back."

Harsh, but I wasn't offended. I didn't blame them. Honestly, I figured I'd probably come back, too. Crime and drunkenness and drug abuse had been almost my whole life. This was how I lived, and I didn't know another way to live. I'd seen true goodness, true holiness, in Mother Teresa and in Father Jim Fratus and in others who had helped me, but I wasn't sure I could walk the path. And it's only by God's grace that I haven't gone back.

That I haven't spent more time in a jail cell. That I haven't been homeless. That I haven't taken a drink or used a drug.

God is patient. God is kind. Christ is there with his open arms, just waiting for us to take that step toward him.

For me, this step included confession — my first since making my first Communion. No, that's not quite right. When I was in MCI-Norfolk, a priest came to the phase unit in which I was lodged. For some reason — a latent religious feeling, I guess, or a brief spark of what later became a fire — I wanted to make a confession.

But I froze. I'd committed some heavy-duty sins, and I sure didn't want to confess any of them to this guy. I'm a criminal! I'm not going to confess to robbing and beating people. So instead I chickened out. I confessed the kind of things that kids confess — for instance, taking the Lord's name in vain. (Not that that's not a sin.) I left all those other sins, mortal ones and venial ones and everything in between, unconfessed. At least for then.

• • •

The Catholic men of MCI-Concord whom I mentioned earlier — Mike, Paul, Joe, and Brendan — weren't the only inmates who urged me along, who encouraged me to find my faith and leave behind the craziness. Some of the older guys, hardened criminals you'd call them, who had done lots of time, were happy for me and my transformation.

They wanted me to get out and stay out. They'd say: "Dude, stick with this. You're a frickin' kid, man. I've been in and out of this place my whole life. You don't want this."

You find this attitude in your fellow inmates especially when you get to minimum security. Guys pull for each other.

Maximum security is just the opposite. It's, "Oh, you're only doing three to five here. You take the knife. You stab him." They
don't want you to get out. Nobody cares about you. But Concord was different. Mother Teresa had told us, "Make this a
place of love." I'm sure a lot of people probably rolled their eyes
when they read that. But there were people who rose above the
squalor and the viciousness of prison and exhibited what can
only be called love.

From Concord, as I mentioned, I was transferred about an
hour and a half down the Everett Turnpike to MCI-Gardner,
and there I was encouraged by a guy named Steve. Steve was
doing life, and, from my understanding of the situation, he was
doing a life sentence that somebody else should have been doing. He got pinched for something that someone else did, and
rather than give him up, he did the time.

I had known Steve from our days in the Charles Street Jail
in Boston. He was a nice guy — very Italian, with a horrible
Boston accent. You can see and hear him as an extra cheering
on the robbers outside the courthouse in the movie *The Brink's
Job*. But Steve was really respected throughout the prison for
taking the rap for a family member. Think about the sacrifice:
to lay down your life for a loved one.

I'm not whitewashing things. Steve was a criminal. He had
grown up in a world where you don't snitch. If you talk, you're a
rat, and life isn't pleasant for rats. It used to be that nothing was
lower than a snitch in that world, though it seems as if everyone
is snitching today. Whitey Bulger, the biggest Boston gangster
of them all, was telling on everybody, giving guys up to the FBI
for years. So it's probably much less likely today that you'd find a
man doing what Steve did. I don't think I could keep my mouth
shut under those circumstances, especially now that I have a

wife and children. Maybe, when I had nothing going for me, I could have taken time for a male relative or even some random guy, but today I have people who count on me, people who look up to me, and I can't imagine them visiting me in prison, believing that I had committed some dreadful crime.

Anyway, Steve encouraged me to stay on the straight and narrow. He'd say: "You don't want to be here forever, dude. This is no life. It's not that it's horrible, it's just … nothing. It's a waste of our life."

Steve knew me. He could tell when I was backsliding. I mean, I wasn't drinking or getting high on the sly, but sometimes I'd still be on the hustle. If I saw a chance to make a few bucks by acting as the middleman in a drug deal, I'd do it. I thought of it as just something I had to do to survive.

But Steve called me on it. He'd say: "Dude, you're going to walk out of here and never have to come back again. Why would you risk that?" He knew that in prison every situation blows up. Every plan goes wrong. It never happens the way you've drawn it up. You think: Okay, this guy's going to get a package, he'll give it to me, I'll sell it to this other guy, and I'll make this much money. Not gonna happen. Because everyone you're dealing with is a criminal and a lifelong screw-up. It's not necessarily that someone is going to cheat you — the old phrase "honor among thieves" has some limited validity, depending upon who the thief is — but somehow, some way, the deal is going to go bad.

Steve knew this, and he knew me, and he cared about my best interests. He saw that I had, or could have, a future, even if he knew that he had none. I'm sorry to say that Steve died of cancer in prison. I still think about him and pray for him.

CHAPTER FIVE
I SHALL BE RELEASED

I was released from prison in February 1990. I'd served only about half of the minimum of my six- to nine-year sentence.

I was scared to go back to Boston. Too many people knew me and my difficulties, and I knew too many bad actors. Could I stay out of trouble if I moved back? I wasn't sure. So I lived for a while in western Massachusetts, close to my prerelease center.

But first I went on tour — illegally.

My brother Donnie's band was breaking big when I was at MCI-Concord. They were Dorchester guys: Donnie, Danny Wood, Jordan Knight, John Knight, and Joey McIntyre. Joey, from nearby Jamaica Plain, was the only one I hadn't known growing up. I told Father Fratus about the New Kids on the

Block, and he went out and bought me a cassette tape of their debut album. It was great R&B, featuring a cover of the Delfonics' "Didn't I (Blow Your Mind This Time)." But it was with their second album, "Hangin' Tough," that they really burst upon the scene.

I was getting sober and hoping for a release at about the time they hit it big. Donnie and I had always been close, even though he's four years younger than me. He had visited me a number of times in prison. Then he and the New Kids did a show for us when I was in MCI-Gardner. The inmates clapped and cheered and went crazy for them. I remember Donnie was wearing these brand-new sneakers, and he traded with me for my old sneakers. I had the sharpest footwear in all of Gardner.

The day I was released from prison, we buried my mother's mother. I attended the funeral. Either later that day or the next — I forget which — I left the state of Massachusetts, in violation of my parole, on a private jet with Donnie. I was going on tour with the New Kids on the Block. It was my first time on an airplane. (And on that private plane I had a lot more leg room and a lot more fun than you do today flying economy class with United.)

Donnie was so happy for me. He got such a kick out of having his brother traveling with him, and I suppose my prison background helped lend a certain sense of coolness or toughness to what people were calling a "boy band." I just know that I was deeply grateful to him for not giving up on me.

We traveled the world, which wasn't the smartest thing for me to do immediately after my release. In prison, however chaotic it was, we were all men, and we had to live by a set of rules. On tour with a band … well, let's just say there were very few rules and fifty million screaming girls. I was trying to make up for lost time, and I made a lot of bad decisions while I was out there, filling the void with meaningless diversions. It's a miracle I stayed sober through it all. By this point, I had been confirmed, but though I was praying, I wasn't attending Mass. I wasn't really seeking a relationship with God.

And I was always envious. Jealous. I felt like I didn't matter. People would literally push me out of the way to get to the famous person. I didn't know who to trust. I was constantly wondering: Does this person like me or is he or she using me to get to someone else? It's hard to find your own identity that far in the shadows.

I moved back to Boston in 1991, first to my own apartment and then to a two-family house that Donnie bought. I lived there with my dad, and the healing started. Or I should say it started and stopped and started and stopped, because we didn't always get along. For one thing, he was still drinking and smoking. Then he was stricken with a pair of strokes. These posed serious physical challenges, but even more they just killed his spirit. He'd been a man's man, and for him to be seen as what he thought was a helpless invalid was a source of shame and embarrassment for him. So he'd just stay in the house. A third stroke robbed him of a good chunk of his memory. Its only upside was that he totally forgot that he smoked and drank. He just stopped doing either one. He never had another cigarette or another drink.

• • •

No Boston guy is fully dressed without his Fighting Irishman tattoo, and I'm no exception to that rule. I got mine in 1990 when Donnie and I went to a tattoo parlor in Los Angeles. We actually ended up on the cover of a German teen magazine flexing our muscles and showing off our matching "Wahlberg Pride" ink.

That wasn't my first tattoo, nor was it my last. I got a Tasmanian Devil on my chest while I was at MCI-Concord. But prison tattoos are done by hand, not machine, and the color would never stay within the borders. Eventually I had it covered by a Boston Celtics emblem. I also have Saint Francis on the nape of my neck and praying hands on the bottom of my right leg in memory of my dad and my sister Debbie.

Then there is my sobriety date — 5-9-88 — on my right bicep. While my actual sobriety date is a little earlier, this is the date when I received my one-year medallion from AA. Greg D, my outside sponsor, drove one hundred miles on May 9, 1989, to deliver that medallion to me in prison.

I saw Greg every week from about the time I decided to pull a con job by making it appear as if I were really interested in getting better and becoming a model citizen. Organizing AA meetings became part of that hustle. I set up the room, I made the coffee, I signed the papers verifying the attendance of the other guys. I had it all covered. But what began as an illusion became a reality.

It may seem strange to read about trying to achieve or maintain sobriety in prison. After all, there are no bars (well, not the kind you order a beer from) or liquor stores inside a prison, and the use or even presence of alcohol is prohibited. But it's easy to obtain booze and drugs in prison, and I used both many times.

When I took the lead in our prison AA chapter, I knew I was putting a target on my back. This probably sounds like typical prisoner paranoia, but I do believe that nothing makes some administrators happier than to disprove a prisoner's claim that he is getting better. They think that the cons are all conning them, and that none of us is really capable of the self-discipline necessary to get straight.

I remember being in the meetings, even when I was hustling, and truly appreciating what an amazing program AA was — for other people. In my heart of hearts, I didn't think I was worthy of its assistance. If they knew what I was really like, I thought, they wouldn't want me here.

I'd hear my sponsor, Greg, who had done time, talk about the changes sobriety had wrought in his life, and it just didn't ring true. It reminded me of when teachers would tell me that I had the potential to be the smartest kid in school, an excellent student with a bright future, and I didn't believe them. I figured they told everyone that. It's their job to give false hope.

I look back now and realize that they were telling the truth, as they saw it. I was a bright kid, but I used all my intelligence to do wrong. It just didn't occur to me to behave differently. And crazy as it sounds, in later years it never occurred to me *not* to use alcohol and drugs. I remember one day walking through the yard at MCI-Gardner and being struck by the revelation that maybe AA really can work, not just for these other more deserving people, but for *me*, too.

Second only to God, Alcoholics Anonymous saved my life.

• • •

It always seems to come back to Dorchester. So it makes sense that I found the woman who would become my wife on my home ground after returning to Boston.

I met her at a community center in the Dorchester neighborhood of Fields Corner, where my parents grew up and where I was born.

The neighborhood has turned over a lot. Once almost entirely white working class, today it has a large Asian community, and on its streets you find Buddhist temples, Vietnamese nail salons, Thai flower shops. Not many of the old faces and names are still around. But I remember them.

I was twenty-five years old and fresh out of prison. I'd spent pretty much the entire decade of the 1980s locked up. I'd done the circuit, from juvenile detention to maximum security prison, and now I was a free man. Just what I was going to do with this freedom, I had no idea.

So I volunteered at an after-school program at the Dorchester Youth Collaborative. Most of the kids were black or Hispanic. There were a few white kids sprinkled in, but they were considered sellouts by a lot of the other white kids — like they'd jumped to the other team.

DYC, as it was known, occupied the second floor of a Dorchester Street building that had been constructed in 1895. It was a safe place in which I could readjust to civilian life as an adult. I was mentoring these kids, doing my best to keep them from traveling down the path that I had traveled. But they were doing way more for me than I was doing for them.

They let me volunteer for two reasons. First, I knew the guy who ran it from my days at the YMCA. Second, Donnie and the New Kids on the Block had hung out there before they really blew up and became famous. They were among those "sellouts" who hung with the black and Hispanic kids. And the thing is, even though they got the label of being a boy band, they were real. They were legit. They hadn't been manufactured in some soulless studio. All but one member of the band was from Dorchester, and this exception was from Jamaica Plain, which was like a cousin to Dorchester. So when the New Kids became one of the most popular bands in the world, they still came back to the Dorchester Youth Collaborative. They wore their DYC T-shirts. They took kids from this place with them around the world. They helped them make music, even helped them make records. They didn't play the big star around here, or put on airs, or act like they were better than Dorchester. Because they *were* Dorchester.

This little community center became famous. It actually attracted fans, sightseers, gawkers. You might show up and find a dozen girls from Holland standing out front looking for Donnie or Jordan or Joey or Jonathan or Danny. It was crazy. And it helped to give the place a real cachet.

At DYC, singing and dancing and creating music were the focus. They kept these kids out of trouble and gave them an artistic outlet that probably didn't exist in any other corner of their lives. These kids came from dangerous places that were plagued by drugs and gangs and violence and hopelessness. They came from Blue Hill Avenue, Geneva Avenue, and Bowdoin Street. Just walking down those streets was nerve-wracking, as you crossed from one gang territory to another, or passed drug dealers and prostitutes and crack addicts.

Almost all of these kids were growing up in single-parent households. Mom — who in ninety-nine percent of the cases was the only parent in the home — might be on drugs. Dad might be in jail. DYC was the one safe haven for these boys and girls. It was the only place they were going to get any supervision, any guidance, any encouragement to be more than what they saw on the streets every day. Heck, it might be the only place they got a decent meal that day.

So they'd come after school, do their homework, have a bite to eat, socialize in a setting without the ever-present threat of violence, and get the chance to exercise their minds and their creative energies. At eight or nine at night, they'd load into a van and we'd drive them home.

DYC was my safe haven, too. And it's where I met my wife.

Benerada Gonzalez, or "Benny" to her friends, is from the Dominican Republic, though she grew up across the river in Cambridge (which, as I like to tell her, isn't really part of Boston). I can't say it was love at first sight. I mean, she was beautiful — stunningly beautiful. When she walks into a room, conversation stops. Everyone looks. But here she was, working with hormone-crazed boys in an after-school program, and she had to be stern and rigid to keep them in line.

So my first impression was that she was a little rough around the edges: a tough girl in a tough place. I wasn't really interested. God only knows what she thought of me at first sight: an ex-con whose roughness extended way beyond the edges.

Our coworkers played matchmaker. They'd tell me that she liked me, and they'd tell her that I had a crush on her. "You'd make a great couple," they kept saying. Finally, we relented. I gave her a call. We talked … and talked and talked and talked. We didn't get off the phone until three the next morning. By the end of that call, I was crazy about her. She was, if possible, even more beautiful on the inside than on the outside.

There was one not-so-small complication. She wore an engagement ring on her finger. Now, none of us at DYC had ever met the guy who gave her the ring, nor did we know his name. But the ring was pretty obvious.

Still, Benny agreed to go on a double date with me and another couple. It was the middle of autumn, time for the famous

Topsfield Fair, a real happening in New England. We spent the day at the fair, seeing the agriculture exhibits and going on midway rides and just enjoying each other's company. It was all very platonic, but I was so into her.

Next came an episode which the meaning of she and I have never quite agreed upon. The day after the fair, she gave the ring back to her fiancé. She said then, and insists to this day, that this return had nothing whatsoever to do with me. It's just that she realized that if she could go out with somebody other than her fiancé and have so much fun, then she probably shouldn't be getting married. This did *not* mean, she said, that she had any particular interest in me.

Needless to say, I saw it then and see it today in a different light. I'd say she was bowled over by my charm and good looks. But as a guy, I would say that, wouldn't I?

Benny knew that I'd been in jail and that I was sober. That's all she really knew at first. But she also knew that I was angry. One time we were out driving, and I pulled into Dunkin' Donuts to get two cups of coffee. As I pulled out a guy cut us off. I went crazy. I rolled down my window and threw my full cup of coffee at his windshield.

Benny was horrified. "Let me out of this car!" she screamed. "Take me home right now. You're an animal. I don't want to be with an animal!"

She had seen the dark side of me: the anger, the hostility, the prison Jim Wahlberg. But as we dated, she saw that I was also capable of kindness, generosity, love. And she helped to bring these qualities out in me.

I gotta be honest here. We struggled. Things were touch and go, and we even broke up at one point. And a couple of months later, we found out that Benny was pregnant with our son Daniel.

I'm kind of an old school guy, as you can probably tell by now. I said no matter what, my kid is *not* growing up without a dad. So Benny and I got back together.

We were together for the first two and a half years without the benefit of marriage, but when we finally woke up and realized we needed to be wed in the Church, I asked Father Jim Fratus to perform the ceremony. Always humble, he said that he would be honored. On October 28, 1995, Father Fratus married us at St. Ann's. Father Jim Fratus, I'm sad to say, died of cancer in 2009. He'd smoked cigarettes like a chimney for years. (I think it was his only vice.) He was just everything a priest should be: patient and kind and faithful. He introduced me to Jesus Christ, which was the greatest gift I have ever received.

Daniel was actually the ring bearer in the wedding. He was the reason that we got married, at least in my mind, and probably in Benny's as well. She may have married me despite not being in love with me. And I'm not sure how much I was in love with her at that moment. I married her more out of responsibility than anything else. Only later, after we began to deepen our relationship with God, did we really fall in love.

Still, our wedding day was special in a million ways, and not only to Benny and me. Donnie and I had grown ever closer since my release from prison and my sobriety. Even during the New Kids' tours, he and I had the kind of honest and revealing conversations that people would love to have with their siblings but seldom do. We really came to understand each other. And on the day I was married, he cried and cried: tears, sniffling, boogers, the whole thing. He was overcome with emotion. He had seen me at my very lowest. He knew how far down into hell I had descended. I was missing from his life. Like the hymn says, I once was lost but now am found. I was like the prodigal brother come home. He'd have killed a whole barn full of fatted calves for me, but just the look in his tear-clouded eyes was enough for me. How I loved him at that moment.

Benny and I honeymooned in Aruba, which is where we conceived the twins, Kyra and Jeffrey. If I was staying for one, I wasn't going anywhere with three. We were a family, and nothing was going to break us up. We settled in for the long haul.

Soon after the twins were born, Benny decided that she didn't want to live in Boston. Like a lot of people from tropical climates, she didn't like our winters. Seasonal affective disorder left her blue in the cold and snowy months. We didn't move right away — but the thought had lodged in my head.

We bought our first home not long after getting married. It was located on Charlemont Street, in a classic Dorchester neighborhood, with a very Irish, stable population. It was the kind of place where, when a house goes on the market, it's not really on the market. Residents let one another know when a house is for sale, and in an informal way they vet and approve potential purchasers. It might sound like a racial thing, but it's not. I mean, my wife is Dominican, and there are certainly black and Hispanic people in the neighborhood who are very much a part of the network. It's just that they want good, hardworking people of any color as their neighbors.

We bought the house off a couple whose daughter I knew. We made the informal contact, and I guess we got the seal of approval. In 1997, we moved in and lived there for two years, with my dad staying in an in-law apartment that we built for him.

Buying that house was a huge moment in my life. I remember the day we closed on it. My wife was working in Boston at the time. So we met midday in the city, did the closing, and then she went back to work while I took the keys and drove to our new home. I went inside, and I just sprawled out on the floor, trying to take it all in. I thought about where I'd come from, what I'd gone through, and how deeply grateful I was to God. I'd been the worst kind of juvenile delinquent — no, that phrase is too mild; I'd been a *criminal* — and now I owned a home in the neighborhood that I once ran through like a tornado. It was such a powerful and emotional moment in my life. I cried like a baby.

It was a God moment. My faith was still in a state of formation (even now I admit I'm a work in progress), but I was overjoyed and prayerful and just so thankful to God.

Our new house was just a couple blocks from the house on Adams Street where I'd slept under the porch as a homeless thirteen-year-old kid. To walk by that every day — to be reminded of what I had been, and where I'd come from — was overwhelming. The house on Adams has been fixed up, but I'll bet that crawlspace is still there — untenanted, I hope. (The Burkes' floor is probably a million-dollar condo by now. Heck, the realtors would probably charge $2,000 a month for my dirt-floor sleeping quarters.)

The Bible tells us to let the dead bury the dead, but though we can put the past behind us, it is impossible to make it just disappear. This lesson was driven home to me shortly after we moved onto Charlemont Street.

There was a grocery store around the corner called the Ashmont Market, the kind of place you might buy a sandwich or cigarettes or a few last-minute groceries. I walked over there one day to grab a couple of items. I ordered a sandwich and was standing at the counter. The woman standing next to me was staring. A typical male, I figured she was checking me out, admiring my good looks.

I smiled at her. "How ya doin'?" I said.

She just looked at me.

"Do I know you?" I asked.

"Yeah," she spat. "You robbed my effing house."

I didn't know what to say. I just walked out of the store. I felt so small I may as well have been slinking home along the gutter. Here I was, a married man with three children, a homeowner, a clean and sober guy who'd put the criminal life behind me, and the past had just popped me right on the nose.

And yes, if the woman was who I think she was, I had indeed robbed her house. Her niece had actually masterminded the job. She told my partner and me that her aunt and uncle were going to be away and where we could find the valuables. But it doesn't matter who the mastermind was. I committed the burglary and was one hundred percent guilty of the crime.

Incidentally, we never did get arrested for it. But I paid a price. A few months after the theft, the owner of the house — the husband of the woman who later chastened me — saw me hanging out on the street corner. He happened to be in the company of a real tough guy, someone no one in his right mind would mess with. Emboldened by the presence of his buddy, the homeowner walked up to me and put his cigarette out in my face. No way was I going to take a swing at him. His associate would have knocked me flat on my butt. So I accepted the humiliation.

A few years later, I ran into the cigarette-wielder at MCI-Concord. Lacking the protection of his sidekick, his attitude was a little different. But then so was mine. I had just knelt with Mother Teresa and her sisters, and I had no interest in making vengeance mine. I'm happy to say that we later ran into each other on the streets — as free men, too. He was sober, I was sober, and we had long since forgiven each other.

While I loved the sensation of being a homeowner, a responsible citizen of Dorchester, I did feel a little sheepish sometimes. People recognized me, and if encounters like the one at Ashmont Market were rare, I did occasionally hear the remark that Kurt Russell's character is constantly hearing in the film *Escape from New York*: "I thought you were dead!"

The rumor mill had killed me several times over the years, I guess, but reports of my death, I am glad to say, had been greatly — well, maybe more like *slightly* — exaggerated.

As I mentioned before, my dad lived with us in an in-law apartment. He'd had a couple of strokes and wasn't healthy. Given our past together — and apart — the fact that he lived with us at all was nothing short of astonishing. But it wasn't as awkward as it sounds, because we had done a bit of healing.

I blamed him (I still do, to be honest) for a huge part of my difficulties growing up. He was, at different times, abusive, apathetic, and absent. But I'd come to understand him, to accept that he, too, had suffered from brokenness, and in his own way he'd done the best he could. He worked hard, I give him that. He was just repeating the cycle of dysfunction.

Our healing wasn't like a TV movie, where we fell lovingly into each other's arms, apologizing for all the hurt and the harm we had caused each other. My dad, being a Boston guy, would say something like: "You were a real bastard when you were a kid but you're okay now. You're a good dad. You're a good guy."

There were even some hugs. Maybe they were twenty years too late, or maybe it's never too late. I earned his respect and ultimately his forgiveness for my many transgressions. I think in his own way he wanted forgiveness as well, and I was able to forgive him.

He and my mom didn't really have a relationship in his later years. Sometimes we could get him to go to a family event, and they'd be cordial to each other. I think my mother forgave my father for his deficiencies as a husband. She said, "I'll always love your dad in my way." She knew the sacrifices he had made. He took on a hard task and did it to the best of his ability. He married a woman with three kids and raised them as if they were his own, while at the same time he was not permitted to raise three of his own kids. That had to be terribly painful. He internalized it. He never talked about it, and we kids never knew what he was going through. His way of dealing with any kind of traumatic situation was to sit at the kitchen table by himself, drinking and smoking cigarettes and brooding. Alone. Utterly alone. Trying in his own way to deal with his pain.

He was even separated from his siblings. My Uncle Archie, who filled me in on a lot of my father's backstory, also had nine kids. Between our families, we could have fielded two full baseball teams and gone at each other. But I barely knew who they were. I didn't even know all their names. That's still strange to me. Your brother and his large family live in the next town over, and you never see them. Not because of some epic quarrel or betrayal, but just because … I don't know. Just because. I know that if I had nine kids and one of my brothers had nine kids, our families would be mixing it up all the time. Our kids would grow up together.

When one of Uncle Archie's daughters, my first cousin, died tragically young, I remember watching how my dad dealt with it. He just sat at the kitchen table, legs crossed, cigarette in hand, drinking and talking to himself.

Dad had no relationship with God. I don't remember him ever talking about God. Maybe he didn't even believe. It's sad for me to think that he took it all upon himself, thinking he had to figure everything out on his own. Like the rest of us, he was ill-equipped to do so. All he did was keep those wheels of dysfunction in motion. That's one of the many reasons I am extremely loving and affectionate with my own children — to the point that I'm sure it's nauseating. Since they were little, I've kissed and hugged and told them that I love them constantly. I never had that, and I desired it so ardently.

• • •

Benny kept at me to move south. She'd lived in Florida for a couple of years as a kid, and she lobbied hard for us to relocate to the Sunshine State. The full-court press was on. I was a homeowner for the first time in my life, but my wife kept revisiting the idea of moving south. Happy wife equals happy life, and I admit that I'm no fan of the cold anymore, either. Plus, I was a married man; I was learning to compromise and to put the well-being of loved ones ahead of my own. I was clean and sober and in such a different place than I'd been for most of my life. So I said, "Sure, honey, let's go."

We sold the house in 1998 and lived in a South Boston apartment while our house in Miramar, Florida, just outside Fort Lauderdale, was being built. We moved in on Valentine's Day 2000. (Meanwhile, back in Boston, Charlemont Street has gentrified. The house I paid $120,000 for recently went on the market for three-quarters of a million dollars.)

The kids were young when we moved, but you can be sure that even in their earliest years I drilled into them a love of all things Boston: its people and its neighborhoods and its sports teams, the Patriots and Red Sox and Celtics and Bruins. No way was I going to raise any Miami Dolphins fans.

All this while, my faith had grown lukewarm. I was still Catholic, but I was also in AA, and I had the AA people telling me I could create my own conception of God. To its credit, AA exalts the concept of a higher power. The program is based in Christianity, but you can believe in whatever you want. They just want you to stop drinking one day at a time and figure out the big picture later.

This inclusiveness, this welcoming environment, obviously appealed to me. I had been a prisoner, the lowest of the low, and yet I was accepted. I will always be profoundly grateful to AA. I still attend meetings. But when you create your own conception of God, it becomes easy to stray from the Church. You can be one of those "I'm spiritual but not religious" types.

So I strayed a bit. We had children and had them baptized, but I wasn't going to Mass. I wasn't going to confession. I wasn't drinking or getting high, either, and I was praying to whatever I had conceived in my mind was God. But it wasn't satisfying because it wasn't real.

And a great reckoning was about to come.

CHAPTER SIX
WALKING TO EMMAUS

I thought I knew pain. I thought I had suffered in my life, living on the streets and cycling in and out of jail. That pain doesn't even begin to touch the pain of finding out you have a kid on drugs. It's a whole different level of pain.

But I guess the story of what we did when we found out that Daniel was on drugs really begins with my reversion to the Faith.

It was 2010. I'd been living in Florida for ten years, clean and sober. From the outside I'm sure we looked like a happy family. I had a beautiful wife, three beautiful children, and a nice home. I didn't drink, I didn't do drugs, and I tried to live a life of service — at least when it was convenient for me.

Part of my wife's strategy of moving to Florida had to do

with getting me away from Boston: the distractions, the temptations, the frustrations. She thought that maybe the distance would give us a chance to focus on our family. But while I was physically present, too often I was emotionally absent. I'd stay in my room for hours at a time watching TV. I had checked out. It's like I had PTSD from the pain and sorrow and shame. It takes courage to look those things in the face and do something about them, and I wasn't up to it.

There was always turmoil just under my surface. I might be great on Tuesday, but I'd explode on Wednesday. I'd storm out of the house on Thursday and make up sweetly on Friday. I saw bits of my dad in me, and I wasn't proud of that.

I was unhappy, and this unhappiness was reflected in my relationships. My wife and I were always arguing about everything — including our faith.

As I said, I'd cooled off and become a tepid Catholic. I believed, but I wasn't exactly on fire. Sometimes I'd go to Mass with the kids; other times I'd drop them off at Sunday school and go home to watch the football games on TV. This was starting to resemble my own upbringing. I was acting for the sake of tradition, because it was something I was expected to do, not because I particularly wanted to be there.

My wife, though, was pushing hard. Benny had been raised Catholic, like most people whose roots are in the Dominican Republic, but her family was hardly devout. Her mom was a seeker: a cradle Catholic who had followed her sister into the Jehovah's Witnesses. But Benny had been caught up in the world like everybody else. She wasn't praying the Rosary or going to adoration or anything like that. She was just attending Mass weekly with her kids and her husband, who was just going along to get along. It was, for me, the path of least resistance.

Then she got invited to a retreat. She went. And she was blown away. She saw the face of Christ. She came home from that retreat and was changed. Really changed. It wasn't some dramatic, fire and brimstone triggered reversal of character. But she was kinder. More patient. More loving. More forgiving. It was tremendously appealing to me. I was really attracted to the post-retreat Benerada.

Benny had always had a temper. Before that retreat, she'd get mad at me, and on cue I'd say I'm sorry, even if I thought she was at fault, because I just wanted to appease her, to get her off my back. I just wanted peace. But now, returned from the retreat, things were different. She wasn't mad anymore. She was at peace.

But she did ask one thing of me: She wanted me to go on a retreat. Not the same one she had been on, which was in Spanish, but a retreat called The Road to Emmaus. Our friend Damaris, who is like a sister to me, also strongly nudged her husband Steve to go. Steve and I said no way. We made a pact with each other. We were *not* going on any retreat. That was final.

You can guess who won that war of wills.

Steve and I did hold out for a while. The date of the retreat came, and we stayed home. I told Benny that I had a God of my own understanding and that was enough for me. Six months passed. The next scheduled retreat drew near.

Then Kyra, my daughter, who was twelve years old, ne to me. She said: "Daddy, I want you to go on the retreat. I nt you to be happy. I want you to know Jesus."

You guys out there know how hard it is to s o to your daughter. It's hard enough when they're just a for some trinket or gadget, but when they're asking y now Jesus? It's impossible to resist. I told her I'd go.

But I wasn't going with an open heart. I was just going to shut up my wife and daughter. I just wanted them to leave me alone, to stop bothering me about this retreat. I figured I could manipulate the situation. Hey, I'd survived almost ten years in prison. Surely I could make it through some religious weekend unscathed.

That's the mindset with which I set out on the Road to Emmaus.

The title of the retreat comes from the Gospel of Luke. Two disciples, one named Cleopas and the other unnamed, set out on their way "to a village named Emmaus" (Lk 24:13). (Some biblical scholars believe that Luke did not name Cleopas's companion so that we could each see ourselves in that place and on that road.)

It is the Sunday after Christ has been crucified, perhaps hours after the stone has been rolled away to reveal an empty tomb. These two disciples are talking about the astonishing events of recent days. A fellow traveler joins them. He asks what matter they are discussing.

"Are you the only visitor to Jerusalem who does not know the things that have happened there in these days?" asks Cleopas, who explains that the women of their group have found this very morning that Jesus of Nazareth was absent from his tomb, and that two angels appeared to tell them that Jesus lives.

The stranger walks with them to Emmaus, teaching and explaining the meaning of the Scriptures. A fire is kindled in their hearts. Upon arrival, the stranger breaks bread with them and says a blessing. Their eyes are suddenly opened. This fellow traveler is Jesus. As soon as they recognize him, he vanishes.

I was Cleopas as I started the retreat, I'll tell you that.

I was wearing a hooded sweatshirt with the hood pulled over my head. I had on my Boston face. Its message to one and all was: "Stay away from me. Don't bother me. I'm not interested in what you have to say."

That whole first day, I kept up what I think of as my Heisman Trophy pose — arm extended, palm out, as if to stiff-arm anyone who gets in my way. But I couldn't leave. My wife would make my life miserable if I did. I'd be taking out a long-term lease on the doghouse. Still, I had steeled myself against being lured into the spirit of the weekend. I would endure it and no more.

Yet no matter how hardened my heart, one of the lessons from AA kept coming back to me: Keep an open mind. Listen to what they say. They can't hurt you.

Little by little, the ice melted. Yes, this was in Florida, where ice always melts, but it wasn't the heat that was melting my frozen heart. Eventually the hoodie came off. The tears were flowing. I couldn't stop crying. I was blown away. (I should admit here that I'm a crybaby. My kids laugh at me for this. We might be sitting in front of the television and on comes the McDonald's commercial in which a kid brings his dad to the Golden Arches, saying, "This is my dad. He's my best friend," and I'll be bawling my eyes out. Yes, I'm a sentimental guy, but the kids don't know that the real reason I cry is because I never had that growing up, and now, through the grace of God, I do.)

Confession was a central element of the retreat. I had made a confession as part of my confirmation in prison, but I hadn't gone to confession again for years. The confession at the retreat was not your typical church confession, in which you enter the confessional, kneel, and whisper your sins to a priest whose face the penitent cannot see. Instead, I was directed to sit in a chair, asked to close my eyes, and told that the retreat leaders would come get me in a while. I waited, wondering what was in store for me. Finally they came, took me by the hand — my eyes were still closed — and walked me into another room. "Open your eyes," they said. I was standing in front of a priest. It was confession time.

I was an absolute basket case. I couldn't stop crying. Through sobs, I began my confession. It was going to be a long one. A *very* long one. But there were thirty guys and just three priests, so I couldn't elaborate too much. I just listed my sins, not their context, and believe me, that took long enough. I tried to keep it to the heavy-duty stuff, but I think ultimately God wants it all. A sin is a sin.

The crazy thing is that a week later, my wife and I were at a party at a friend's house, and I saw the priest to whom I confessed. I've never been so thankful in my life for the seal of the confessional, which is the absolute and inviolate secrecy and confidentiality pertaining to one's confession.

I returned from the retreat a changed man, just as my wife had returned from hers a changed woman. I had the undeniable feeling of the presence of Christ in my heart. I was on fire. Everywhere I went I saw signs of Jesus. I committed to one hour a week praying in the presence of the Blessed Sacrament. As I was driving home after making this commitment, I heard a buzzing noise. I looked up and saw a plane and read the sky-writer's message: God Loves You.

Jesus had saved me. There is no other explanation. And my wife led me to Jesus. She pointed me in that direction. She knew that he was the great healer and that he could redeem me. She knew that I could find peace in his mercy. She wore down my resistance, and when my daughter pleaded with me … well, it was all over.

• • •

Everything was coming together after the retreat. I was so hungry for God. This was the feeling I'd been searching for all my life, and that I foolishly thought I could find in drugs and alcohol.

And then … we found out that my 16-year-old son was on drugs.

I admit it: I was mad at God. I said to him: "You finally got me. I go to this retreat, my heart melts, I open up my life and my heart to you, I dedicate myself to your service, and this is what I get?"

It crushed me.

But then I realized: I didn't have to go through this alone. I had God. With him by my side, I could deal with it. I couldn't do it without him. I can't even imagine trying to do it without him. But with him … all things are possible.

So I continued to pray. I continued to serve. I continued to go on retreats. And all the time, things at home were falling apart. From the day we ordered Daniel to pee in that cup, things got progressively worse.

He was arrested numerous times for marijuana. He was thrown out of multiple schools for the same offense. One of these was an alternative school where they watch your every move. It's foolhardy to try to put anything by them. Yet Daniel tried, and he got caught.

The principal called me, crying. Yes, the principal cried. He said: "I can't believe this. Your son was arrested today for smoking marijuana. He's afraid that you're not going to go down to the police station and get him."

"He's right," I replied. "I'm not coming. He needs to understand that actions have consequences."

In my mind, there was no way I was going to pick that kid up from the police station. Let him spend the night in jail. That'd teach him a lesson.

But the principal straightened me out. "I've been working with troubled kids for thirty years, Mr. Wahlberg. Your son is a good kid. I don't know why he's getting high. But I'll tell you this. If he gets locked up with bad guys, he's going to become one of those bad guys. Don't let them put him in jail. Just come get him and figure it out."

I did. But we didn't figure it out. Instead, we continued on the merry-go-round of arrests and rehab and sober homes and AA. Daniel learned quickly how to get away with things. When he was on probation, he passed his urine tests with flying colors — probably because it wasn't his urine.

At home, our lives were turned upside down. He continued to steal from me, to smoke weed, to sneak around. His younger brother and sister were being affected by the fallout. Finally, Benny — not me, but Benny — put her foot down.

"He's got to go," she said. "We've got to be strong."

I didn't think I could do it. Throw my own son out of the house like my dad had done to me? True, I wasn't evicting him during a Boston winter, but still, I was reluctant. Finally, the day came when we threw his stuff into a green garbage bag and I said, "Dude, you've got to go."

Daniel started crying. "Please, Dad, don't. Please don't."

Scenes from my childhood flashed before my eyes. I was sure that this was the right thing to do. Maybe my parents had been sure, too, when they tossed me out?

I overrode whatever reservations I may have had. I told myself that if we just let him stay home and get high, then we'd be part of the problem.

"You gotta go, Daniel," I said, and I literally pushed him out the front door, closed it behind him, and locked it. Then I fell to the floor and started crying. Just sobbing an ocean of tears. I was a complete mess. I had thrown my son out of the house, just as I had once been thrown out of my house.

In my despair I hit upon a plan. I'd go with him. Forget my wife; I had to save my son. We'd get an apartment together and I'd protect him and get him off drugs.

God didn't allow that to happen. He strengthened me. He lifted me up, got me off my back and onto my knees. Over the coming weeks Daniel would call us, crying, saying, "I've got nowhere to go," and beg us to let him come home, but we stayed firm.

Then he got arrested again, in July 2010. He was a juvenile, so he was released into our custody. It was the Fourth of July, but we were not celebrating Daniel's independence. Instead, I was driving him from Fort Lauderdale to a treatment center in Rhode Island.

My cellphone rings. It's my wife. She's at home watching EWTN's *Life on the Rock*. Four guys from a place called Comunita Cenacolo, a Catholic faith-based community for addicts, are giving their testimony. It's powerful. "That's where Daniel needs to go," she says. "My son needs God. My son needs Jesus Christ. He doesn't need any of this other stuff."

She went online, did the research, got a phone number, and dialed. The bishop of Birmingham, Alabama — Bishop Robert Joseph Baker — answered the phone. Benny told him our story. He listened patiently and urged her to call Albino Aragno, who came from Italy to start a Comunita Cenacolo in St. Augustine, Florida. He was a drug addict who had lived in the community in Italy and has spent the rest of his life serving others.

Albino set up a visit for us. For three consecutive days, Benny and I dropped off Daniel in the morning and picked him up after dinner. We stayed in a hotel. For these three days Daniel was accompanied by a "guardian angel" who showed him around, though he was expected to pitch in and perform the necessary work of the community. So he spent those three days raking leaves and sweeping floors and otherwise engaging in manual labor in the company of young men who were in various stages of their walk with Christ.

After three days we met with Albino. "Do you want to live here?" he asked Daniel.

"Yeah, I do," replied Daniel.

"We'll take him," said Albino. "Bring him back in two weeks."

Two weeks? Are you kidding? That's the worst thing you can tell parents of a drug addict. There was no way Daniel would still agree to go after a two-week delay. And this wasn't some summer-long program, some vacation rehab spa. Comunita Cenacalo requires young people to spend three years in work and prayer within the community.

Even if Daniel did agree to it, three years felt like insanity. I thought: "Daniel needs to get on with his life. What's he going to learn to do in three years? Clean toilets and grow vegetables? How is that going to help him get a good job, buy a nice house, become a good middle-class American consumer? And what are people going to think? What are they going to say about *me*? About *my* failures as a parent?" I should have realized that more than anything, my son needed God.

Daniel assumed that he'd be staying with us for those two weeks. I said no. We'd schedule the requisite doctor's appointment for him and help him get his passport, which he would need, as part of the road to recovery takes place in Italy. But he wasn't going to stay with us, and I told him frankly that I didn't think he'd follow through and enter the program, either.

Two weeks went by. It was time to leave. Daniel said he couldn't go. He was working on some guy's album, and the guy had already paid him money, and blah blah blah. We rescheduled; he blew it off again. Albino called. He told us that either Daniel was there on Monday or the offer for him to join the community would be withdrawn.

We relayed Albino's message to Daniel. Sunday night he showed up at our house, suitcase in hand. Early Monday morning we got in the car, and I drove while Daniel slept. I was driving as fast as I could. I pulled into the community. The members came out and surrounded the car, in a loving and curious way, for they don't get many visitors.

I woke Daniel. He panics. "Take me to the store," he said.

"Sorry, son, you're here. Get out."

He did, and I left.

That night Benny and I slept soundly for the first time in a very long time.

• • •

Comunita Cenacolo was founded in 1983 in an abandoned house in the town of Saluzzo in the Italian Piedmont by a little nun named Sister Elvira Petrozzi, or Mother Elvira. She welcomed the lost, the marginalized, the drunken, the drugged. Her ambitions were modest, but Divine Providence had other ideas. From that one home on a lonely hill, Comunita Cenacolo has grown to include seventy-five houses in twenty countries, including Italy, Croatia, Costa Rica, Poland, Portugal, Liberia, France, Spain, the Philippines … the list goes on and includes four homes in the United States.

Mother Elvira modestly says: "Everything happened without me even realizing it. I dove into God's mercy and I rolled up my sleeves to love, love, love … and serve! I am the first to surprise myself with what has happened and what is happening in the life of the Cenacolo Community. It's a work of God, the Holy Spirit, and of Mary."

The name *Cenacolo* — Cenacle — refers to the room in which Mary and the apostles gathered after the Crucifixion. Mother Elvira explains: "Mary was there with the apostles, closed and full of fear after the death of Jesus. They were just like today's shy, mute, and scared youth. Her maternal presence gathers them together and helps them to pray. The Holy Spirit comes down with the strength of God and they become courageous witnesses. We called it the Comunita Cenacolo (Community of the Cenacle) because we want this same transformation to take place in the hearts of the young people whom we welcome."

Bishop Robert Joseph Baker brought the community to America. As a priest, he was studying in Rome, at the Angelicum, the Pontifical University of Saint Thomas Aquinas, and he began asking people what our faith was doing for addicts.

"You've got to meet this crazy old nun," he was told. And so in 1992 he was introduced to Mother Elvira. They communicated over a long period of time. "Keep praying," she urged. "Keep praying."

Father Baker, who was then pastor of the Cathedral-Basilica of St. Augustine, received a piece of donated property in Florida in 1993. Mother Elvira sent two men, Franco and Massimo — drug addicts who did not speak a word of English — to start a community there. After a long struggle it flourished, despite its unorthodox methods.

You see, families pay *nothing* to send their young men (ages 18-40) and young women (18-30) to the Comunita Cenacolo. The community lives completely off Divine Providence. It takes no money from the government. It takes no tuition money. It doesn't run car washes or sell raffle tickets or send its members out to panhandle. I can testify, as the father of a Comunitarian, that they will never ask you for a dime. But Divine Providence, acting through the grateful and the generous, sees to its needs. Friends of the community give donations of money and goods. The community, in turn, donates its excess to others.

When Daniel entered the community, he spent his first year in St. Augustine before being sent to Italy. Daniel lived in two separate Italian communities and also in a community that was perhaps a football field's length away from the spot where, in 1981, teenagers saw apparitions of the Blessed Virgin Mary in Medjugorje, Bosnia and Herzegovina.

Prayer, hard work, and friendship are the cornerstones of the community. There are no therapists. There are no medications dispensed. You have to be young and hardy enough to work all day. You say three daily Rosaries as well. You wake up, you eat breakfast, you pray a Rosary, and you go to work. You break for lunch, you eat, you pray a Rosary, and you go back to work. You work till day's end, you eat dinner, you pray a Rosary, and you go to sleep.

You take one shower a week, although in summertime you are permitted more. There's no hot water, though. There are no locks on the doors. You work the land, planting and harvesting. You eat what you grow; there is no Walmart around the corner.

You pray, and pray, and pray some more. At the end of the day you are exhausted.

You are forbidden to say the following things:

- I'm too busy.
- That's not my responsibility.
- I don't like it.
- I don't feel like it.
- I don't care.
- I'm tired.
- I can't.
- Mind your own business.
- I'm not capable.
- Leave me alone.

Parents are not barred from the community during the three-year commitment, but they can't just show up. There is an annual retreat and an annual Festival of Life, both of which parents are encouraged to attend.

Six months into Daniel's stay, Benny and I went to the first retreat. We were amazed. Daniel looked and sounded great. What we didn't realize, of course, was that if you take a kid, any kid, who's on drugs and require him to eat well, work in the hot sun, and refrain from drug use for half a year, he's going to be, or at least appear to be, a new man. Add to that the fact that he's regurgitating everything he hears and the parent, desperate for hopeful news, rejoices. It's a miracle! My son's a saint! I want to take him home and show him off to everybody!

Then we saw him six months after that. He was still doing

great. But a month later we got a call from Albino: "Your son wants to leave."

I got on the phone with Daniel. And he sounded like the same person I had dropped off a year earlier. It was like the devil had him by the short hairs on his back and was not going to let him go.

"What are you going to do?" I asked. "Where are you going to go? You can't come back here. You're on probation. Would you rather go to jail than stay at Comunita?"

He said, "Yeah, I'd rather go to jail than stay here another minute. I hate this place."

It was the devil talking through him. I hung up the phone. I was overwhelmed. What was I going to do? How was I going to fix this? I got in the car with no definite idea of where I was going, but I ended up at church. It was as if the car was driving me. I walked into the chapel with the Blessed Sacrament, and I knelt down and prayed.

I'm weeping, I'm praying, I'm handing everything over to the Lord. I'm there for an hour, maybe two hours. I have no concept of time. My phone is in my back pocket and it keeps vibrating. Finally I take it out and have a look. There is a string of texts from my wife and a barrage of calls from a number I don't recognize. Just what I need right now: robocalls. Another call comes in from the same number, and to stop this nuisance, I answer. It's my son. Two hours out of community, and he's already got a cellphone.

"Dad, I made a mistake. I'm going back. They're coming to pick me up."

Instead of trying to fix this myself and screwing it all up, I had placed this in God's hands. My despair turned to joy.

Daniel went back. We didn't hear from him again for

months. Not a peep. As they say in community, no news is good news.

Another year passes. It's time for him to go to Europe. He goes to Italy in February, and that summer Benny and I travel to see him and experience the Festival of Life, where thousands of people converge on Saluzzo, that small town in the Piedmont region. People are testifying, witnessing to the miracles God has performed in their lives. Perhaps a hundred priests are hearing confessions. It's an extraordinary experience.

The next step in Daniel's Comunita journey was called verification. He came home for two weeks so that we could verify where he was in his walk. We were nervous. Every time Daniel would use his cellphone or hop on the computer, my wife would panic. Who's he calling? What's he up to? A mood of dread and unease pervaded the house.

Finally, he came to us. "I know there are rules. You tell me what they are and I'll follow them."

"I don't want you contacting anybody you used to get high with," I told him. "I want you to spend time with us or with your friends that we know to be good people. I want you to enjoy yourself, Daniel, but you know we're afraid. You haven't been here in a long time, and the last time you were, the cops were here."

There was no drama for that fortnight. It was great.

Daniel returned to Europe — to Medjugorje, to be specific, the site where it is believed the Virgin Mother has appeared. Comunita Cenacolo encourages family members to experience the community in-depth once the son or daughter has fully integrated, and I was eager to see him and to visit Medjugorje. My visit came as a surprise to Daniel; he walked into the office one day and there I was.

was all over.

• • •

Everything was coming together after the retreat. I was so hungry for God. This was the feeling I'd been searching for all my life, and that I foolishly thought I could find in drugs and alcohol.

And then ... we found out that my 16-year-old son was on drugs.

I admit it: I was mad at God. I said to him: "You finally got me. I go to this retreat, my heart melts, I open up my life and my heart to you, I dedicate myself to your service, and this is what I get?"

It crushed me.

But then I realized: I didn't have to go through this alone. I had God. With him by my side, I could deal with it. I couldn't do it without him. I can't even imagine trying to do it without him. But with him ... all things are possible.

So I continued to pray. I continued to serve. I continued to go on retreats. And all the time, things at home were falling apart. From the day we ordered Daniel to pee in that cup, things got progressively worse.

He was arrested numerous times for marijuana. He was thrown out of multiple schools for the same offense. One of these was an alternative school where they watch your every move. It's foolhardy to try to put anything by them. Yet Daniel tried, and he got caught.

The principal called me, crying. Yes, the principal cried. He said: "I can't believe this. Your son was arrested today for smoking marijuana. He's afraid that you're not going to go down to the police station and get him."

"He's right," I replied. "I'm not coming. He needs to understand that actions have consequences."

In my mind, there was no way I was going to pick that kid up from the police station. Let him spend the night in jail. That'd teach him a lesson.

But the principal straightened me out. "I've been working with troubled kids for thirty years, Mr. Wahlberg. Your son is a good kid. I don't know why he's getting high. But I'll tell you this. If he gets locked up with bad guys, he's going to become one of those bad guys. Don't let them put him in jail. Just come get him and figure it out."

I did. But we didn't figure it out. Instead, we continued on the merry-go-round of arrests and rehab and sober homes and AA. Daniel learned quickly how to get away with things. When he was on probation, he passed his urine tests with flying colors — probably because it wasn't his urine.

At home, our lives were turned upside down. He continued to steal from me, to smoke weed, to sneak around. His younger brother and sister were being affected by the fallout. Finally, Benny — not me, but Benny — put her foot down.

"He's got to go," she said. "We've got to be strong."

I didn't think I could do it. Throw my own son out of the house like my dad had done to me? True, I wasn't evicting him during a Boston winter, but still, I was reluctant. Finally, the day came when we threw his stuff into a green garbage bag and I said, "Dude, you've got to go."

Daniel started crying. "Please, Dad, don't. Please don't."

Scenes from my childhood flashed before my eyes. I was sure that this was the right thing to do. Maybe my parents had been sure, too, when they tossed me out?

"Papa, what are you doing here?"

For the next two weeks, Daniel served as my guardian angel. I don't speak Bosnian, Croatian, or Italian, the primary languages of the region, so I relied on Daniel for everything. He translated the Gospel for me and interpreted conversations. We worked side by side in the daily life of the community. We cried together and we prayed together and we experienced true healing.

I apologized to him for my part in his troubles. Believe me, I was not a perfect father. Daniel saw me taking a lot of it onto myself.

He said: "Dad, what are you talking about? This is not your problem. This is not your fault. You were a great dad. You've always been kind and loving and caring. You showed me the right things to do. I just didn't want to do them."

He was being too kind, too generous, but I appreciated it. And as strange as it sounds, I thanked him for being an addict. All that he had been through, all the pain, all the suffering, had brought our whole family to the foot of the cross. This is the most important thing in our lives, and his tribulations had delivered us.

As his three years came to a close, Benny and I visited him.

"I want to stay," he told us. Comunita Cenacolo stages a play called *Credo* (The Creed) and tours it around Europe. Daniel wanted to travel with the play, which depicts the life, death, and resurrection of Jesus Christ. He worked on *Credo*, and then he spent another year in the community, his fifth.

The natural temptation, after your son or daughter has been gone for five years and emerges clean and sober and off drugs, is to invite him home and shower him with all the gifts you were not able to give during his absence: "You're so amazing! You look great! You're healed! I want to give you a car! I want to give you a leg up on a career!"

Comunita recommends against this. They don't want young people to return to the scene of the crime; they want them to go out into the world and be men and women of Christ.

Now, if another member of Comunita comes to you for help, that's okay. If one of Daniel's compatriots says, "Mr. Wahlberg, I understand that you're into production work. I'm interested in that. Do you think that maybe you could help me out?" I'd help him or her in a second. You can be of service to others — but not your own.

So Daniel moved to Boston and lived in a rectory with daily Mass and the Blessed Sacrament available to him. It was all there for Daniel during his transition year.

Today, three years after leaving Comunita Cenacolo, Daniel lives with my mother in Boston. Alma is in the early stages of dementia, and Daniel is one of her caregivers. He is so kind and so patient and so loving. I'm so proud that he is my son. Drawing on his experience with *Credo*, he also works for the stagehands union in Boston.

Mom will say to me, "Oh, that son of yours. He's so good. It's all because of you." And I'll gently correct her. "No, Mom — it's all because of God."

The miracles — and I don't use that word lightly — that this community works in these young people are awe-inspiring. Consider the case of John Young, a friend who today works at a Christian residential school in the African country of Liberia.

This isn't the first time John has lived in Africa. Addicted to drugs, he got clean during his five years with Comunita, after which he asked to work in the community's mission house in Liberia. John made a three-year commitment. After a year,

Ebola broke out. The Comunita main office told its people in Liberia: "Look, we understand if you want to close the mission temporarily and come back when the threat is over. Nobody will judge you. This is a fatal disease and a very scary time. People are dying, and nothing you can do will save them."

The missionaries replied that they would pray on it.

In the meantime, John's father called and ordered him home. John's response, in essence, was this: "I'm not going home. I am home. Dad, these children have already been abandoned. I can't leave unless I bring all fifty children with me. I can't abandon them. I work for God."

John stayed all through the Ebola outbreak. He survived. This guy had been Sid Vicious — a punk rocker heroin addict, very far gone — and here he was risking his life to stay with Liberian orphans as Ebola raged throughout the region.

After his mission John came home for a brief time, but he's back in Africa, working in a school. I talk to him every Thursday. As is often said with respect to Saint Augustine — the saint, not the city — the biggest sinners can make the greatest saints.

CHAPTER SEVEN

FIGHTING THE SCOURGE

C omunita Cenacolo didn't only save my son's life; it also affected me in profound ways. It sent me running to confession, and it motivated me to take on this important work of raising awareness so we can help people find healing from brokenness and addiction. For me, this has taken the form of public speaking and making movies with an emphasis on addiction and giving witness to God's mercy.

From my perspective, there is only one path out of brokenness, and that path is God. Only God can take all of these negative things and turn them into assets. In my case, he uses me to let people know that there is a way out of the hell of addiction and brokenness.

It's like he said to me: "Your message is going to have depth and weight because you lived it. You will be able to reach broken people because you had the same kind of brokenness. You'll be able to reach their families by telling them what happened to you and what happened to your family. You know what it's like to have an alcoholic dad. You know what's it's like to be an alcoholic yourself. And you know what it's like to have a son who is an addict like you."

I've never been the shy sort, and I don't really get nervous talking in front of large groups. A thousand people in the audience? No problem. Parents, adults, church groups? Fine. But I get a little nervous addressing high schoolers. I remember what it was like to be a teenager and have an old guy come in to talk to us. It goes in one ear, out the other.

I'm always more comfortable when I'm talking to a faithful audience because we have Jesus in common. But even with secular audiences, I will talk about God. Hey, they gave me the microphone; I'm going to tell them what I really believe. If they have a problem with that, then they don't have to invite me back. Even in public schools, I will ask the organizers where I might find a room in which to pray before I speak. I tell them they're welcome to join me. Sometimes they do.

I know that God is always and ever present — even when I have the microphone. I remember the time I was asked to speak at a Catholic conference for men. The invitation came maybe six months or a year before the event, so I said I'd do it and didn't think much more about it till the time drew near. I was going to give my testimony, which I know by heart. After all, I lived it. But still, I feel as if I'm doing the audience a disservice if I don't prepare, so on the plane to the event I put pen to paper to sketch out my remarks in some detail. I was ready to rock.

I arrive at the conference. Then I make the mistake of looking at the brochure the organizers have given me. It lists the other speakers. My heart sinks. They are bishops, theologians, holy people, and other wise men.

Oh, man. What am I doing here? I'm overwhelmed, filled with dread and fear. I start to shake — visibly. I don't know if other people can see it, but I can feel it. There are two speakers still ahead of me, but I'm too nervous to enter the hall and listen. Their eloquence and learning will only make me feel worse. I'm in absolute despair. I'm going to make a fool of myself up there.

I see confession stations throughout the hallway. I slip into one. "Father," I say, "I'm supposed to speak at this thing in a few minutes and I'm afraid. I don't know what to do."

"That's the devil," says the priest. "I've read your biography in the program. As far as I'm concerned, you're the one who belongs here speaking. You can actually testify firsthand to God's mercy. Not second- or thirdhand, but firsthand. God saved you from the hell you were living and the path you were on. Tell them what God has done in your life. These other speakers, they were raised with the Faith. They were smart, they were educated, they had advantages. They studied these things; you lived it. Go tell what you have seen and lived."

I am emboldened. I bolt from that confessional ready to tell the world. I'm not afraid anymore. I feel God's presence. I am dressed in his armor. Standing in the hallway, waiting my turn to speak, I hear the voice of God saying, "Don't be scared. All you have to do is tell them the truth."

It's time for my talk. I'm walking through the long hallway, past tables and vendors and toward the hall. I see my hand go up — involuntarily; it just happens, without any conscious thought on my part — and land on a kid's shoulder. He's a young black kid, and there aren't many black people at this event.

I say, "Hey man, how you doin'?"

He turns around. He's honest with me.

"I'm not doing well. Actually, I was just leaving."

"What are you talking about? It's only halftime. There's a lotta time left on the clock."

"I dunno," he says. "I'm struggling with my faith. I just don't feel like I belong here."

We talk for a couple of minutes. I say, "Brother, will you do me a favor?"

He asks me what the favor is.

"Will you sit somewhere I can see you? I'm really nervous. It'd be great to see a friendly face. Somebody I can talk to."

He agrees. He sits where I can see him. And without pointing him out, I tell the crowd what just happened with the priest and with the kid in the hallway.

The young man stayed for the whole program. He spent the rest of the day with me. A couple of weeks later I was headed to the Festival of Life in St. Augustine, the great weekend-long celebration of the Comunita Cenacolo. I asked him to come to the community, and I was blown away that he said yes immediately. He didn't know me, but he trusted in the Lord. I got him a flight and a hotel room. The honorarium that they gave me for speaking turned out to be exactly the price of his flight plus hotel.

At the Festival of Life, there were miracles everywhere we looked. Young people who were lost but now were found; who were dead but now were leading their families to the foot of the cross. Some were becoming priests, some were becoming nuns. Giving their lives to missions, to orphans, to the service of God.

The young man, Marcus Butler, is still in my life.

. . .

Before I took up residence in Walpole State Prison, I had never known a person who died of an overdose. Not one. Yet now I visit schools — elementary schools, even — and when I ask a crowded auditorium of five hundred children how many know anyone who has died from an overdose of drugs, typically more than half will raise their hands. That's just mind-blowing. Where did this great emptiness, this profound brokenness, come from?

South Boston was ground zero of the opioid epidemic. It started with OxyContin. Guys have been robbing drugstores since time began in Southie, but in the early 2000s they turned it into an art form. The Southie kids weren't robbing for money, they were robbing to get high. They looked down on the poor souls who stick needles in their arms. They wouldn't get high that way. But when they couldn't get the Oxy anymore the pain was so great that many suicides followed.

That was the beginning. Since 2013, well over ten thousand people — most of them young or in early middle age — have died of opioid-related overdoses in Massachusetts alone. It started in poor communities and then spread into middle class and even affluent sections. It's not just poor people anymore.

It saddens me to say that one reason the crisis hit South Boston so hard was the decline of the Catholic Church as the lifeblood of that community. Partly this is related to the more general and tragic turning away from the Faith that is happening in so many places, but it's also a function of the scandals that rocked the Church in Boston — the kind of thing explored in the movie *Spotlight*.

I didn't want to see that movie. I figured it was just another sneering anti-Catholic broadside from Hollywood. I mean, Hollywood isn't exactly making *Boys Town*-type movies these days. Spencer Tracy is long gone. But I went to see *Spotlight*, and I'm afraid that it rang true, given what I know of the situation within the Boston archdiocese. Even the most faithful Catholics in Boston admit that the problem of priests molesting young boys was of a sickeningly large scope. And Southie was hit especially hard. As a result, the Church lost much of its moral credibility just at the moment its people needed her most.

This was terrible timing. But in spite of the scandals, the Church has to do more — a lot more — for the addicted and their families. The scandals don't change the fact that this is the Church Jesus Christ founded. This is the Church that has the Eucharist, the true presence of Christ on earth. We're called to bring light to the darkness of addiction. We cannot allow the disgraceful behavior of some priests and members of the hierarchy to dim that light.

Three years ago, I was asked to speak at a candlelight vigil on Overdose Awareness Day in a small city outside Boston. I arrived to find a moving sight: a thousand or so purple flags planted on the spacious lawn in front of city hall, representing each person who had died of an overdose in Massachusetts the previous year.

I hadn't adequately prepared myself for how I would feel when I saw those flags blowing in a gentle breeze on a candlelit evening in Middle America. I was just overwhelmed. I looked around and saw a Catholic church nearby. I felt a tremendous sense of relief. I went in to pray, to get myself together, to ask God for direction for the right words to say to the families gathered on this lawn — all these hurting people. I emerged feeling his presence.

The crowd is really filling in, and I see representatives from a variety of churches and faiths. But I don't see a Catholic priest. I'm getting concerned. I have a Catholic Mass finder app on my phone because I travel a lot. I find the phone number of this local church and make a call. After punching in what seem like about twenty extensions, I reach the parish priest.

"Hey, Father, this is Jim Wahlberg. How you doing?"

"Fine, fine. What can I do for you?"

"Well, I'm outside. In front of the church, with all those purple flags. There's a candlelight vigil for overdose victims about to start. I see all sorts of ministers and whatnot out here but there's no priest. Now, maybe I'm selfish, but I'd kinda like my guy to be out here, too. So Father, why ain't you here?"

He gets defensive. "Hold on. We've done plenty for families. Do you know how many young people we've buried?"

I tell him he is missing the point. We go back and forth, and I apologize to him if I seem too aggressive, but the bottom line is that he is sitting in his office, not fifty yards from the flags, instead of being out here with all these hurting people and families.

"We weren't invited," he says.

"Well, I'm inviting you."

A minute later this six foot five guy in his mid-thirties who looks like a professional football player but is wearing a Roman collar comes out. I go over to him.

"Hi, Father, I'm Jim. I'm sorry if I seemed rude over the phone. If I knew you were this big I wouldn't have pressured you."

He laughs and says it's okay. When I get up to speak, I invite him to come up and say a prayer. I want him to stand up for our faith. He does. Everything is cool.

The next year I'm invited back. I go straight to the church, because I have no business speaking in front of other human beings unless I'm getting some direction from the Lord. Believe me, if I'm on my own up there, glorifying myself, talking about how awesome I am … well, I'm not awesome. There's nothing awesome about me. The smartest thing I ever did was get on my knees.

And that's what I want to do before I speak at this second Overdose Awareness Day. There's only one problem: the church doors are locked. It's 5:00 p.m. The event starts at seven. So I get on my trusty app again, call the church, and tell the woman who answers the phone that I'd like to come in and pray but I can't get in.

"We're closed," she says.

"But I really need to come in and pray."

"You can't. We're not open."

I'm starting to lose my cool. "Didn't you hear what Pope Francis said?" I ask. "He said, 'Open the doors.' The very least we can do is unlock the doors of the church. Let's just start there."

I'm standing on the steps outside the church, and I see the priest approaching, walking with a fellow priest. He smiles.

"Hey, Jim. We're here. So you're not mad this year, right?"

"Well, Father, actually … "

I tell him I'm a little bit upset that the doors are locked. I need access. I need to go to the source. Where are people going to pray and worship when they're broken, when they need to feel the presence of God, even though it's after working hours?

He explains that there have been problems with crime and break-ins in the neighborhood. I tell him that I understand, that I'm not minimizing those concerns, but that perhaps he could station someone to keep vigil at the church, as is done with adoration of the Blessed Sacrament. You work off a schedule, and you stay till the next person shows up. If the next person doesn't show up, you stay until someone comes. You don't leave Jesus alone.

"You've got to make it work, Father," I plead, in what I hope is a respectful tone. "You can't shut the doors of the church."

(I think he got mad at me again. There goes that crazy Wahlberg …)

But this is an annual event now. The priest is an invited speaker, and he shows up every year.

This is one priest — a good priest — in one parish — a good parish — but the story highlights a broader problem. As a Church, we Catholics have done a poor job addressing the opioid crisis. Too often we are reactive, not proactive, when it comes to offering people help and healing from addiction. We wait for them to come to us — and then half the time our doors are locked shut.

So let's start by making sure that people have access to Jesus. Access to the Blessed Sacrament. Locking doors doesn't make us "safe" — it shuts off Jesus from those who need him most. He, and not a metal bolt, is the true source of our safety.

• • •

Though I haven't made a film based on my story or my son's story, I have made ten films about addiction.

The first movie I produced, *A Feeling from Within* (2012), was really just another hustle. I figured hey, this isn't rocket science. I just need to surround myself with talented people and work hard. And that's what we did. My buddy Michael Yebba and I cowrote the film. Michael, who has been my writing partner on several projects, is a street kid from the projects of South Boston. He was one of those lost South Boston kids who was robbing drugstores. He and I met, we clicked, and he wrote a script based on his own experiences.

The subject of this short movie is addiction. The main character, an addict, wakes up from an overdose and thinks he's in rehab, but it's really purgatory. I put together an impressive cast and I think the movie works, but I made a mistake with the rawness of the language. It's realistic, but it greatly limits the audiences to which I can show the film. Schools and the sponsors of drug summits tend to shy away from movies with profuse f-bombs. And if you can't reach kids, what's the point?

I didn't make the same mistake with *If Only* (2015), which Michael and I wrote and Michael directed, and for which Danny Wood of New Kids provided the original music.

My son Jeffrey, who has since been featured in a range of films, most recently as Diego in *Dora and the Lost City of Gold* (2019), played a high-school kid whose best friend dies with a needle sticking in his arm. He's a young man seeking acceptance who starts experimenting with drugs. *If Only* doesn't have a happy ending, but then neither do most real-life stories of drug addiction. Michael and I have no interest in making preachy, didactic, eat-your-spinach films. We just want to contribute to awareness, to dialogue, to the sense of hope and possibility that is essential to any recovery.

So many people are out of control, lost, dying. I've met so many good people who come to me and say they've lost a child or a spouse, a brother or a sister, to this scourge. I had to do something, using whatever talents God has given me, and drawing on my experiences, both degrading and redemptive.

Michael and I also cowrote *The Circle of Addiction* (2018), my directorial debut, which follows a series of young people who are sinking ever deeper into the pit of addiction. Raising the money for that production was such a refreshing experience. Usually a producer is selling people a bill of goods when he asks them to invest in his movie. He tells them what a handsome profit they'll make if the movie makes money — which is a huge if. But in this case, I walked into offices and said, "There is absolutely no chance that you are ever going to get your money back." The only promise I made was that it would be a good movie that would educate people, especially young people, about addiction, and not in a preachy or obvious way. They wrote checks; we made the movie.

We shot the film in Manchester, New Hampshire, a region that has been devastated by the opioid epidemic. We had done an Opioid Youth Summit in the Granite State, and I knew we had a lot of resources we could tap into, and we did. For instance, there are real DEA agents in the film's drug raid. They came to the location in their masks and never took them off. When they finished the scene, they got back into their cars, identities still concealed, and sped off.

We had access to the courthouse, the jail, the police chief, the fire chief. All these people — real people — volunteered for the project, because they are living through this epidemic. They've seen friends, neighbors, and loved ones die. You're hard-pressed to find someone who hasn't been affected by this pestilence, especially in rural areas, small towns, and working-class neighborhoods of this country.

Each of us has something we are called to do. I feel as though God is calling me to make these films, to start these conversations. Every time I think about moving on, about walking away, I remember the families that have lost loved ones — their grief, their forlornness, the sadness in their eyes. Who am I to walk away?

I don't claim to have all the answers. But if we pray with each other, communicate with each other, and love each other, I have to think we're on the right path. We're opening up avenues for change.

The Drug Enforcement Agency (DEA) has sponsored a number of my talks and screenings. (If you'd have told me thirty or forty years ago that I'd be involved with the DEA today, I wouldn't have been surprised, but I'd have been shocked to learn that we were on the same side.) New Orleans, Baltimore, Salt Lake City, Louisville, Albuquerque, Charleston — the DEA sends us wherever the scourge of opioids is ravaging a city.

Boston is an exception, for absolutely maddening reasons. A representative of the mayor's office came up to an event we held in Manchester. We had ten thousand people there. Jeff Sessions, then the Attorney General of the United States, showed up. So did the governor of New Hampshire, a whole set of celebrity athletes, and others. The mayor's rep was really impressed. He told me that they wanted to hold a similar event in Boston, with a screening of *If Only* and inspirational talks by some of the same people who spoke in Manchester.

Great. We'd love to. But then I get a call. The showing is off. It seems that they have a problem with the movie.

"What is it?"

"There are too few people of color in *If Only*," he tells me. "It's almost all white kids!"

"Our public schools are filled with black and brown children," says the mayor's rep. "They're not going to identify with this movie."

I was disgusted. This struck me as flat-out racism. Give these kids a little credit, will ya? They understand the issue, and they're capable of empathizing with people who are damaged in this crisis, whether their skin is white, black, red, brown, or yellow.

• • •

I've had so many people come up to me after screenings of these films and say, "This is exactly what happened to us." But not every post-screening encounter is as affirming, and that's okay. After a showing of *If Only* in San Diego, two mothers came up to me, quite upset. They disliked the scene in which a mother of a young man who will eventually OD rudely dismisses another mother who tries to warn her of the path her son is on. They said it seemed like she didn't care, and they were here to tell me from firsthand experience that mothers, even those who might seem hard on the outside, *care.*

Of course they do. The mother in my film isn't supposed to be unfeeling; she just assumed that a tragedy like this could never befall her family. After all, her son was perfect. He'd never use drugs. He was immune to those temptations. A lot of people think that about their kids. It's not that they don't care, they just can't believe this epidemic could touch their own families.

But I sure wasn't going to argue with those two mothers. They had lost their children. They're entitled to say what they will. Their suffering is greater than any I can imagine and any I ever hope to bear. I told them that if I'd offended them in any way I was sorry, because that was not my intent.

I'm frequently moved to tears by the stories people share with me after these screenings. I recall one striking instance, though I forget which town it was in. I have a habit of watching the kids as they file into the auditorium. On this occasion a tall, good-looking boy in a varsity jacket caught my attention. This kid was movie-star handsome, right down to the layered, feathered hair. He just looked like he had everything going for him.

So we screen the movie, I take questions, and then as we break up a line forms to have a word with me. This kid is way back in line. As he draws closer, I notice that he's crying. When he reaches the front of the line, I see that he's not just sniffling or softly weeping; he's really crying. His face is all red and swollen. I don't know what else to do, so I put my arms out and hug him.

Between sobs, he whispers in my ear: "My dad is a drug addict. My mom threw him out of the house. He just got arrested. It's so hard. I just don't know. … "

He kept crying and crying. He couldn't stop. Finally he pulled himself together and asked if we could get a picture. Sure. He ducked into the bathroom to wash up, came out, we took the picture, and I never saw him again. But I've wondered now and then what has happened to that young man. I pray for him. And for his mother and his drug-addicted father.

That episode also reminded me not to make snap judgments. My first thought had been, "Man, if I were that good-looking in school I never would've gotten in any trouble." But the young man's life was upside down.

You never know whose life you might touch. When I'm speaking I pick out one or two people in the audience who seem really tuned in and I try to reach them. I've had listeners who appear to be totally disengaged, as if they could not care less and are just waiting for this to end so they can get back to something they care about, and yet they'll come up to me afterwards and say, "That was incredible. Thank you so much."

You just never know. That's why you can't write people off. You can't assume that you know what they're thinking.

We are living in difficult times. But there is hope. If a scoundrel like me … if a sinner like me … can find redemption, so can you, no matter what your circumstances may be.

Don't give up hope. Even if you or your spouse or child or a loved one is held tight in the grip of addiction, don't give up hope. But don't give them money, either. Don't buy them drugs. Don't be part of the problem. Be part of the solution.

I am a believer in tough love. We did it with our own son. And he came back and told us that if we hadn't done the things that we did, he'd be dead. He would have never stopped getting high.

The first thing we need to do, which is what I'm trying to do with my addiction films, is to shine a light on the problem. To expose the secrets. To break the code of silence, which is especially strong among the Irish I grew up with. We have to get over this whole we-ain't-talking-about-it thing, because people are burying their kids. Burying people they love. And none of us is immune or untouched.

The important thing isn't laying blame. It's taking the necessary steps to correct the problem. This requires frankness, honesty, conversation — and God. Each of us, I'm sure, would step in front of a bullet for our kids. So why are we so shy about speaking with them about the lethal danger of drugs and alcohol and opioids?

Again, this is where the Church can and must do more. There is a vacuum here that only God's love can fill. More and more when I go to Mass I hear in the prayers of the faithful a prayer for people who are addicted, or whose loved ones are addicted. I have a real appreciation for that, because I know the power of prayer.

Each of us, in his or her own way, can play a part in this healing. Father Jim Fratus opened the door to Christ for me. You and I can do for others what Father Fratus did for me; we can lead the broken and the addicted toward the light of Christ. We can open the Church doors and welcome them in.

Many times after screenings, I've gone back to my hotel, flopped on the bed, and cried my eyes out. Someone asked me the other night if I ever feel like giving up. Of course I do! Who doesn't? All this sadness and brokenness and death. The opioid epidemic just seems to be getting worse. As our society turns its back on God, we drift ever further into hopelessness.

Nobody said this road was easy. I just keep moving forward, trying to keep the conversation going. I feel like giving up all the time. But I won't. God has chosen a path for me, and I'm scared not to follow it.

• • •

My most recent film about addiction, *What About the Kids?* (2020), is faith-based, a story of a family seeking and finding answers after a young mother dies of an overdose. It is also the first of my addiction movies in which I make clear that God is the solution.

What God had in store for all of us making this movie was incredible. I knew enough to know that I couldn't just go out and make the movie. There are a lot of off-camera matters that have to be done right. First up: I wanted to shoot this film on holy Catholic property. So I went to a friend, a Boston guy (funny how often that happens) who works for the Archdiocese of

Miami. I asked if we could use the Madonna Retreat Center, which used to be Madonna High School, a Catholic school for girls. He got me in to see the parish priest, who told me it was his last day — he was retiring — and that as far as he was concerned, I could do whatever I wanted. So I went up the chain of command and had lunch with Archbishop Thomas Wenski, who welcomed me to use the retreat center. God put it on my heart to ask the archbishop if he'd consent to appear in the film (nothing ventured, nothing gained), and he said yes.

Then I arranged to have priests on the set and daily access to the Blessed Sacrament. First thing in the morning, every day of the shoot, we went to Mass at the church next door. Not everyone did. It wasn't mandatory, and not everyone working on the film was a Catholic. But this was a deeply Catholic film, and I wanted the atmosphere on the set to reflect that fact.

The music in *What About the Kids?* was written and performed by members of Comunita Cenacolo: addicts who have been healed through Christ, and who now use their talents and treasures to give glory to God.

And do you remember Marcus Butler, who entered my life when I was speaking at that conference and somehow (I believe by an act of God) my hand found his shoulder? He called me about a month before we were going to shoot the movie. He said: "Man, I'm really struggling. I've been running the youth group at church but I just ... I don't know. You're doing all this speaking and stuff ... maybe I could tag along with you? Maybe you could mentor me?"

To me, that was a courageous act. One of the most difficult things in my entire life has been to ask another man for help. This kid was doing just that; he thought I had something to offer. I told him about the Catholic-themed movie I was making and invited him to come down. He said, "I don't know anything about making movies." But I told him we'd find something for him to do. He agreed and showed up on the appointed day. We prayed together, and he worked with us. He did everything we asked of him. He brought life. He brought joy. He brought peace to people.

Marcus wasn't the only person on the set who was struggling with his faith. A friend of mine, Kevin King, had just been fired from his job. He'd been brought up Catholic but had fallen away from the Church. I said come on down to Florida and help us make a movie. He, too, protested that he knew nothing of making movies, but I told him, hey, I don't know anything either. Just come and we'll figure it out. I put Kevin together with Marcus. They worked together, they explored their faith together, and … we'll see. It's a long journey.

Even my wife worked on this film, running the craft services and catering department. Now, Benny has no interest in Hollywood whatsoever. She won't go to the movies with me because she objects to the immoral content of so many contemporary films. R-rated movies are strictly off-limits for her. But because *What About the Kids?* is so steeped in Catholicism, she consented to help — and she did a great job.

Perhaps the biggest "God moment" in making this film came with casting the grandmother. If you're familiar with her previous work, her name may come as a surprise: Patti D'Arbanville. Her career stretches from being an Ivory Soap baby to her role in *The Sopranos*, and includes a wide range of movies, including several very risqué parts in films by Andy Warhol in the 1960s, among others.

A casting agent put me in touch with Patti. I was looking for an older woman and an eight-year-old girl. When I told the agent it was a faith-based film she said: "I've got just the actress for you. She's crazy about God. She yells at me when I eat meat on Friday."

I was intrigued, obviously. Patti and I spoke. She told me she'd had a conversion six years earlier and was sick of doing what she called "filth." She wanted to do something meaningful. I told her my movie was about God's mercy and redemption, about forgiveness and healing. Based on a couple of conversations, I offered her the role. And then not long after, I made the near-fatal mistake of going on YouTube and looking at some of her work. Yes, she was a terrific actress. But this was very raunchy stuff. Not pornographic, but full of foul language and sexual situations.

I couldn't sleep a wink that night. I was tossing and turning and kept hearing the profane lines from YouTube. What was I going to do? I couldn't tell her she couldn't do the movie because of other stuff that she had done. She'd had a conversion. God's mercy, redemption, forgiveness: I had to live it, not just talk about it.

But I worried that maybe her presence in the film would draw fire. And what about Our Sunday Visitor, which was underwriting the film? I had to be responsible to them. I couldn't just light their money on fire.

The day after this sleepless night, I called a friend, a Catholic movie producer who was behind the pro-life film *Unplanned*. I said, "Mike, I need your advice." I told him about the steps we were taking to base this movie in Catholicism: Mass every day, Eucharist available, the cooperation and even participation of the bishop. I told him that I was completely committed to Patti for this part, but that some might find her previous work objectionable, and I wasn't sure how to handle the situation. What if the folks at Our Sunday Visitor objected to her involvement?

He said, "Look, Jim, if they believe in God's mercy and redemption and forgiveness, all will be well. Call them and see."

I did so, using as a pretext my desire to bring them up to date on different aspects of the production. I spoke with Jason Shanks, the head of Our Sunday Visitor's film department. I rattled off an account of where we stood with respect to this and that, and then I told him that for the part of the grandmother in the film I had signed a really talented actress who had done work that was raw, gritty, rough. Not pornography, but not Christian by any stretch of the imagination. I was not contractually obligated to clear the casting with Jason, but I didn't want to start off this relationship with OSV on the wrong foot.

Jason listened. "Great," he replied. With her in the movie we can reach more people. We can talk about the power of conversion. We can demonstrate just what God can do in someone's life. He never even asked me her name. I was so proud to be working with people like that.

And I was so proud to make that film with Patti: a humble, gracious, talented woman. She received the Sacrament of Confirmation. She goes to Mass daily. She prays the Rosary regularly. She wants to proclaim Jesus.

So we had veteran professionals like Patti working with an ensemble that included other professional actors, some regional actors, some very talented amateurs and local South Florida performers, and, of course, Archbishop Wenski.

The archbishop is used to writing his own lines — at least when he's not reading from Scripture — but I made bold to write his lines for the film. I wanted him to say, "We need to do more," not only as a society but as a faith. We need to do more to take care of our sick, our addicted, our hopeless. He spoke the lines and added a prayer.

With the archbishop, I was dealing with a man who was used to taking a leadership role. He's not only a man of God, he's also a man's man who smokes cigars, rides a Harley, and speaks something like seven languages. He wasn't used to taking orders from a director. Here he was, on his own turf, so to speak, speaking to a couple hundred people in the pews and yet he was not in charge. But he was a good sport, and the charisma he exudes in everyday life came through in the film.

Not everyone was on board with the overt Catholicism of *What About the Kids?* I actually had one fellow, a well-known Protestant evangelist, virtually beg me not to depict the grandmother praying the Rosary in the final scene of the film. It would turn off non-Catholics, he said, and limit the reach of the movie. Sorry, buddy — it's my movie, and the Rosary stays.

That doesn't mean that this movie, or my work in general, is for Catholics only. It just means that I'm not going to hide my faith, or water it down. Catholics have taken it on the chin now for quite a few years, partly for the priest scandals but also, more generally, as the country as a whole and the media in particular exhibit open hostility to our faith. Don't believe me? Then try expressing your Catholic view of abortion on social media.

I believe that Christians of all stripes should work together to provide healing and direction for those suffering from addiction. We need to express our faith and live our faith. We also need to love one another, as Jesus taught us. We need to lift one another up, support one another.

If our neighbor tells us that his son has cancer, we respond in a variety of loving ways: We cut his grass, we bring over a casserole, we offer to run errands, and we pray. But if our neighbor tells us that his son is addicted to drugs, we flinch. We tell our kids to stay away from that house. We might even shun the neighbor and his son in the grocery store. We think he's a bad kid and that his mom and dad are bad parents. We cast blame instead of love.

Yet the beginning of an effective response to addiction and its ultimate end is found in love. The love of God, and our love — however difficult it may be at times — for one another.

CHAPTER EIGHT
A WORK IN PROGRESS

Time is a funny thing. It's like an eraser, but it can never really erase what matters. Sometimes I forget where I've been, what I've been through. It's hard to recall it all. It seems as if it happened to someone else, maybe someone up on a movie screen. Not only was everyone else in my life convinced that I was going to spend the rest of my days in jail or end up dead on the street, *I* was convinced of it. I was, literally, hope*less*: without hope. Those same people are shocked and amazed by my life today, and so am I. If God can work miracles with a sinner like me, he can do the same for anyone.

Yet despite it all, sometimes I still doubt the power of God. I doubt what is possible through him. Until I am reminded.

For instance, my Emmaus group, consisting of the men on

the retreat that led to my reversion, still gets together once a week. One of the men from the retreat recently came to the rest of us and explained that he had legal problems and was going to be appearing in court. He said he'd really appreciate it if a couple of us showed up.

We did. But it wasn't a couple of us, it was fifty of us, dressed in our Emmaus shirts, which are white and emblazoned with a cross and a rose. There were so many of us that the judge assumed we were there for the prosecution, not the defense.

The prosecution showed a videotape of this man's crime. And it went far beyond mere "legal problems." He had participated in a violent assault, captured on a home video surveillance camera. Though he never pulled a trigger, another man did, and someone was shot and wounded. It was, essentially, a shootout between criminals. It was ugly.

The prosecution was seeking a sentence of up to fifteen years in prison. The judge, assessing the nature of the crime and the incredible turnout in support of the defendant, addressed us. He said (and I paraphrase): "So all you guys are here for him. Interesting. You want to know something? Everybody that comes to my courtroom charged with attempted murder finds God. Every single one. This is nothing new for me."

The defendant was granted a continuance. The case would be taken up a week later.

The night before the next court date, I visited the defendant, my Emmaus brother. There was no doubt in my mind that he was prison-bound. How could he not be? I'd seen the video. He was obviously guilty of a serious crime. And the judge, while impressed with our turnout, had made sarcastic cracks about the case. The only question was how much time he was going to serve, and whether he might be deported. (He was a native of Panama.) I thought the only way I could be of service to him was to tell him what to expect in prison: how to behave, what to do and what not to do, how to survive the ordeal. So that's what I did over dinner — his last supper as a free man, I assumed.

The next day, seventy-five of us showed up in court, wearing our Emmaus shirts. The judge was taken aback. He acknowledged the large crowd and addressed the defendant: "If I even considered giving you a break, it wouldn't be because I think you found God. It would be because I know these men are prepared to keep you accountable and to show you a better way to live. They're prepared to mentor you. These guys took a day off from work — twice — and by my count there are more here today than the last time."

The judge gave him house arrest and probation. Manny walked out of the courtroom and into the sunshine rather than into a police car that would take him to prison. It was incredible.

We, the men of the Emmaus retreat, walked out of the courtroom, stunned. We dropped to our knees and said the Rosary in the hallway of the Broward County Courthouse. How dare we doubt the power of God! How dare we doubt what is possible with him!

What a lesson this was for each of us. No matter how blessed we have been, when the going gets tough, we too often look to ourselves. What am *I* going to do? How am *I* going to fix this? It overwhelms us; it consumes us. The stress is just too much. It causes me to lose weight and whatever is left of the hair on my head.

I should be taking it to God. Whatever is going to happen will happen, but I won't have to handle it alone. That reassurance, that comfort, is so beautifully powerful. When I forget about trying to do it all myself (and invariably screwing up) but take it to him instead, the truth will be revealed. It sure was that day in court.

Here's another example, this one even closer to home — literally. Benny and I were recently getting the house ready for our Fiat Group, a monthly dinner meeting of Catholic couples. It was our turn to host. Benny had just had surgery and shouldn't have been doing any lifting, so I told her that I'd move the furniture while she supervised. If you've ever been in a similar situation, you know what's coming.

"Don't move that there."

"Why?"

"Just don't. Move it over there."

"It's better here."

And so on. The usual husband-and-wife disagreement over where stuff goes escalated into a shouting match.

I said, "I'm outta here" and left. She called me on the cell phone and unloaded. "I'm sick of you. We're hypocrites. I don't want these people coming over. This is not how Christian people behave."

I turned the car right around and came home. We stood face to face.

"We're canceling tonight," she said. "If these people knew …"

"Who do you think is coming over here tonight?" I responded. "Do you think these people don't argue and fight with each other? Do you think they don't sin? They don't make mistakes? Can't you see what's happening? The enemy is at work. The devil doesn't want twenty people here tonight talking about his enemy, Jesus. He doesn't want us praying and reading the Gospel. He wants us at each other's throats. He wants to divide us."

We calmed down. This time I was the one who saw what was happening; usually I'm the one who is blinded and Benny is the one who sees. Rarely are we both strong at the same time. I lean on her, and she leans on me.

We hosted the meeting that night. Two dozen or so of us met and read the Gospel and prayed for the sick and prayed for our marriages. It was a God-centered night.

• • •

I haven't had a drop of alcohol in over three decades. Occasionally, I admit, the thought of having a drink is subtly alluring. When you have bad wiring, like I have bad wiring, that temptation never completely disappears. Maybe I'll be at a football game and think: "Dude, you've been sober for thirty-two years. You could probably have a drink now. What's the big deal? It's just one beer. You're just being sociable."

But God instantly reminds me of my past. He gives me a glimpse of what used to be. Because, I swear, every time I have that thought, I see someone in the crowd, usually someone next to me or in my row, acting like a drunken fool, embarrassing himself and causing others to feel a mixture of pity and scorn. It happens every time. If I'm at a Red Sox game, there's always somebody sitting in front of me that gets up twenty-five times to get beers, stumbling and staggering from about the fourth inning on. I say a little prayer for him or her and thank God for being so kind as to remind me that this is a temptation I can't afford to indulge.

Even when I receive the body of Christ, I never go to the chalice for the blood of Christ. I'm in no position to take that risk.

I know that the voice inside urging me to take a drink is the enemy. The devil. He's asking, "How can I get you not to be a godly man? How can I get you to make a choice based on self-ishness and not based on God or the needs of others?"

Because of my last name, I have access to movie premieres, big sporting events, things like that. My friends are always asking me to get them into the hot parties at the Super Bowl, which I attend every year. I'm happy to do so, but after a few minutes at the party, I tell them I have to go to the bathroom and I just leave, because I find it difficult to be around drunken people. They remind me too much of myself.

Before I moved to Florida I did what I thought was an ample amount of preparation as an alcoholic man. I went to AA meetings and mentally prepared myself for my new surroundings. Alcoholism and drug addiction are, in part, about an absence of community, of connection, of love, of friendship. And I was headed to a place that was far from the web of friendships and connections I had built over the years of my new sobriety.

We move to Florida. New house, new town, new state. Nobody knows who I am, and I don't know who they are. I'm isolated. If I want to, I can re-create myself. They don't know my past or my struggles. So there comes a time, maybe a year or two into our lives in Florida, when I don't want to go to AA meetings anymore. Hey, I'm cured. I don't need this. In fact, I bet I could start drinking again — responsibly this time.

I'm sitting in an AA meeting thinking these dark thoughts. I'm going to start drinking like a gentleman and not come back here. AA has been a great help to me, but I just don't need it anymore. I'm not angry; I'm just ambivalent. I feel no compulsion to come back, and I figure — and this is always a warning sign — that I could do it on my own, without anyone's help.

Then Lisa raises her hand to speak. Lisa is an angel to me. She's probably about seventy years old, but she's not exactly a grandmotherly seventy. She's lived a tough life, and it shows. I'm sure she was a real looker in her day, but she's been beaten and abused, and she bears the scars. Yet for all this, there is an indomitable quality about this tough New Yorker. Lisa may be crazy, but she's no quitter. She's got spunk and spirit and mettle.

She speaks her piece, and the meeting breaks up. My last meeting — or so I think. As we adjourn, ready to go our separate ways, Lisa comes over and gives me a big hug, with passion. Wow, where did that come from?

I hug her back and she whispers something so outrageous in my ear that I break out in a fit of laughter. It is wildly inappropriate, yet in Lisa's own way it's so innocent and well-meaning that I think, man, I gotta come back tomorrow to hear what she's going to say next.

I drove home, laughing all the way. I hadn't laughed that hard in a long while. As if by — I hesitate to say *divine intervention*, given what she said, but it sure seemed like that — the thought of not coming back to AA just left me. And it's never returned.

Lisa was an angel, a crazy angel, I guess, who may have saved my life.

• • •

Sometimes the Wahlberg family saga seems so strange that it can't quite be true. I mean, my family goes from being an anonymous if enormously large clan, broke and rowdy and wracked by alcoholism and probably looked down upon by most of the people in our immediate neighborhood, to a nationally known brand and, in our home state of Massachusetts, virtual royalty.

But believe me, we're still the same people we were all those years ago. Mark and Donnie are rich, no denying that, but at heart all the members of my family are still working-class Dorchester people. As I'm writing this, I'm preparing to go to my brother Bob's twenty-fifth wedding anniversary. The party is being held at a local firefighters' hall. We're not Four Seasons kind of people.

When you have nine kids who have grown up in dysfunction, things aren't always going to be peaches and cream for them as adults. We have our quarrels and unpleasant moments like any other family has. Sometimes relationships are strained.

Yet we all know that God has blessed our family. Members have been extremely fortunate. No one will deny that there's been an element of luck involved, or of being in the right place at the right time. That a broken working-class family could produce two of the biggest pop-music stars of the 1990s, and one of the biggest movie stars of the twenty-first century, and a national restaurant chain as well, is … well, it's a miracle.

Even today, when I walk the streets of Dorchester, it occurs to me as I pass people in the street that I might have robbed them back when, or I might have broken into their homes. I'm not being dramatic. I'm not proud of it. I'm absolutely ashamed of the person I used to be. But God pulled me out of it. He said: "Here's what we're going to do, son. We're going to take all of your deficits, all of the nasty little things about you, and make them assets. You are going to go out and talk about the terrible things you used to do and how I healed you."

It's not about me being a great guy. Because, to be honest, I'm not a great guy. I might get in my car this afternoon and when somebody cuts me off, I'll give them the one-finger salute. I'm not consciously trying to do that; it's just that if I don't have time to process things, to ask myself what a servant of God should do, I react — and my immediate reaction is almost always the wrong thing.

I'm a flawed man. A sinner. But I've been blessed as the husband to an amazing woman and the father of three amazing children who have never seen me drink. I also won — or "won" — the trifecta: I was raised by an alcoholic, I became an alcoholic, and then I raised an addict. But my faith, and the steps I took to grow and heal from this condition, enabled me to find healing and then to be there for my son, and to learn from him, too. His addiction brought my family to the foot of the cross. What greater gift could there be?

I am hardly a finished product. I remain a sinner. I struggle to know God's will, but I try to obey God's will as best I can. I try to be the best husband I can be, the best father I can be, the best example of my faith that I can be.

I didn't have those examples growing up. But I do have the examples today of other men living godly lives. They've shown me what it means to be a dad, to be a contributing member of a community, to be a faithful servant. To the extent I can succeed at marriage, at fatherhood, at being a man of service, I owe my success to my relationship with a loving God and my sobriety.

I am walking and talking evidence of the healing, redemptive, and merciful powers of Jesus Christ.

This is my mission. It's the mission of any follower of Jesus. If we want to bring healing to our addiction-plagued world, then we need to step up. We need to let people know about Jesus. It's as simple as that. Your story may not look like mine. Let's be real — it almost certainly doesn't. But you have something important to offer. Don't hide your light under a bushel basket. And if that thought scares you, just remember: Nothing is too big for God.

Nothing.

No matter how big your sin is, no matter how far down the scale you have fallen, no matter how wrong a life you may have lived, God can heal you. You can rise above that. You can be a man or woman of God and a person of service. You can be what God intended you to be.

Now go be it.

ABOUT THE AUTHOR

James Wahlberg is the founder and CEO of Wahl St. Productions and has been working in and around the field of addiction recovery for more than 25 years. Jim's personal experiences with recovery and commitment to his faith led him to create a number of short films on the topic of addiction, including the critically acclaimed *If Only* that is particularly relevant in light of today's opiate crisis. *If Only* was created to encourage a dialogue between parents, teachers, faith leaders, and young people; and it has been shown to hundreds of thousands of people in venues ranging in size from classrooms to arenas. The Spirit continues to guide Jim in his journey of recovery and to help others find hope in an often seemingly hopeless situation. He and his family are active members of St. John XXIII Parish in Miramar, Florida.